P9-BBU-510

MAC & CHEESE

80 Classic & Creative Versions of the
ULTIMATE COMFORT FOOD

BY ELLEN BROWN

PHOTOGRAPHS BY STEVE LEGATO

Running Press
PHILADELPHIA · LONDON

Copyright © 2012 by Ellen Brown
Photographs © 2012 Steve Legato
Published by Running Press,
A Member of the Perseus Books Group

All rights reserved under the Pan-American and International Copyright Conventions
Printed in China

*This book may not be reproduced in whole or in part, in any form or by any means, electronic or mechanical,
including photocopying, recording, or by any information storage and retrieval system now known or hereafter
invented, without written permission from the publisher.*

Books published by Running Press are available at special discounts for bulk purchases in the United States
by corporations, institutions, and other organizations. For more information, please contact the Special Markets
Department at the Perseus Books Group, 2300 Chestnut Street, Suite 200, Philadelphia, PA 19103, or call
(800) 810-4145, ext. 5000, or e-mail special.markets@perseusbooks.com.

ISBN 978-0-7624-4659-9
Library of Congress Control Number: 2012930287

E-book ISBN 978-0-7624-4683-4

9 8 7 6 5 4 3 2
Digit on the right indicates the number of this printing

Cover and interior design by Amanda Richmond
Edited by Kristen Green Wiewora
Food Styling by Ricardo Jattan
Prop Styling by Mariellen Melker and Amanda Richmond
Typography: Verlag, Archer, Strangelove and HT Gelateria

Running Press Book Publishers
2300 Chestnut Street
Philadelphia, PA 19103-4371

Visit us on the web!
www.runningpresscooks.com

The love and support of a wonderful family is even more comforting than a bowl of mac and cheese.

This book is dedicated to Nancy and Walter Dubler; Ariela Dubler, Jesse Furman, and Ilan, Mira, and Lev Dubler-Furman; Lisa Cerami, Josh Dubler, and Zahir Cerami; and David Krimm and Peter Bradley.

TABLE OF CONTENTS

ACKNOWLEDGMENTS

While testing recipes and writing a cookbook is a solitary venture, transforming it into a tangible object to hold in your hands is always a group effort. My thanks go:

To all the talented chefs around the country who devised some truly delicious renditions of mac and cheese, and were willing to share their recipes.

To the many members of my vintage grapevine of food professionals who tipped me off to some of these chefs whose dishes I didn't know, with a special thanks to John Mariani, my dear friend and the best restaurant resource in the country, and to Christine Chronis, with whom I've swapped food lore and recipes for decades.

To Kristen Green Wiewora, who is a national treasure in her role as my editor at Running Press.

To Amanda Richmond, the talented designer at Running Press who made these photos so dramatic and enticing, and whose design makes this book a delight to hold.

To Steve Legato, as good-natured as he is talented as a food photographer.

To Ricardo Jattan, the food stylist who made all these dishes stunning, and to Curtiss Bazemore, who assisted him and never complained about another trip to the market for more cream and butter.

To Mariellen Melker for finding all the wonderful props used in these photos.

To Ed Claflin, my agent, for his constant support, encouragement, and humor.

To my many friends who critiqued my work as they wondered if they would ever eat a dish in my house again that wasn't mac and cheese, including Constance Brown, Kenn Speiser, Fox Wetle, Richard Besdine, Vicki Veh, Joe Chazan, Kim Montour, Nick Brown, Karen Davidson, and Bruce Tillinghast.

And to Patches and Rufous, my wonderful feline companions, who kept me company from their perches in the office and always hoped that a few crumbs of cheese would fall on the kitchen floor.

PREFACE

Back in the summer of 2011 when Hurricane Irene was barreling up the East Coast from the Carolinas to Maine, the United States Coast Guard posted a document online titled "72 Hour Suggested Hurricane Supply List." At its core were sensible foods packed with nutrition that needed neither cooking nor refrigeration. But after the dried fruits, cans of fish, and granola bars there was a category called "comfort/stress foods." Some examples in this section were cookies and sweetened cereals.

Although those two foods are hardly what pop into my head, what struck me was the recognition—even by a buttoned-down government entity—that food is far more than the fuel to power our bodies with vitamins and minerals. It nourishes our emotions, too.

And one of the most comforting foods, for physiological and psychological reasons, is mac and cheese. It shows up on every poll of comfort foods, and was selected twice in a row by The Food Network as the "Comfort Food of the Year." If you look at the categories of foods in magazines' year-end "Best of" issues, you'll often spot mac and cheese on the list.

Comfort foods protect us from a threatening world. Their appeal is based on nostalgia, and the time of our childhood when life was far simpler than it is today. My memories of mac and cheese are of a homemade dish. It never came from a box, although the Kraft blue box had been on supermarket shelves for a decade by the time I was born. But the mac and cheese wasn't made with the imported Cheddar and Gruyère that fill my refrigerator today, either. It was made with Velveeta. Back then Velveeta, albeit a color and texture that never existed in nature, was the "gold standard" for mac and cheese, and for grilled cheese sandwiches—another great comfort food.

"Real" cheeses like Swiss and Muenster were reserved for sandwiches on crusty rye bread from the bakery, not Pepperidge Farm white. Velveeta was also comforting because it was known, and because it made mac and cheese soft.

Our sense of taste actually comes to the party late in our reactions to eating and food. First we eat with our eyes, and then the sense of smell enters into the equation. Our muscles prefer foods that don't make them work very hard, which is why soft foods like mac and cheese, meatloaf, and mashed potatoes get high marks.

The brain kicks into the reaction shortly thereafter. Sugar and starch produce serotonin, a neurotransmitter that increases the sense of happiness. Replicating its effect is what makes antidepressants like Prozac work. Salty foods like potato chips make the brain release oxytocin, a hormone also triggered by sexual satisfaction.

While these are physiological responses to food, the brain also generates our concomitant emotional responses. Certain foods, especially those eaten in childhood, have specific memories associated with them. There was the chocolate pudding that you had on Sunday afternoons at your grandmother's house, the snow cones at the county fair in the summer, and cookies with lots of frosting at Christmas. These connections also explain why foods we logically know to be inferior in nutritional value, like Hostess Twinkies, remain on the market decades after real bakeries have popped up all over the country. And why everyone has a personal definition of what side dishes are appropriate for Thanksgiving dinner.

While our attitudes to categories of food are hardwired into our brains, our attitudes about specific ingredients do change with time and with experience eating a panoply of different foods. While I will always love mac and cheese, no longer can it be made with Velveeta. My palate is too far advanced now.

That's where the recipes in this book enter your life and kitchen. You'll be able, when cooking the dishes in this book, to relive the warm memories of the mac and cheese of your youth, but satisfy the tastes you like today, too.

Happy Cooking!

Ellen Brown
Providence, Rhode Island

INTRODUCTION

After World War II the United States became the world's cultural capital. From the movies made in Hollywood to the Abstract Expressionist art shown in the galleries of New York, the country's art led the way. But American food remained a stepchild for decades longer. The menus of the lauded restaurants were written in French, with an occasional outpost of Italian beginning in the 1960s.

American food was viewed as an offshoot of tourism. You ate tacos in Tucson, clam chowder in Boston, and crab cakes in Baltimore. While wonderful cooking went on in millions of homes around the country on a daily basis, "frou-frou French" was what white tablecloth restaurants served, along with a hybrid called Continental Cuisine. Humorist Calvin Trillin once quipped that the continent in question must be Antarctica because all the food had been previously frozen.

It's now been more than three decades since the country celebrated its bicentennial, and we've seen the birth and flourishing of New American Cuisine. Such trailblazing chefs as Larry Forgione, Alice Waters, Paul Prudhomme, and Lydia Shire laid the foundation for American food made with the finest ingredients, with mac and cheese as part and parcel of that cuisine.

There are recipes for mac and cheese dating back to medieval cookbooks, including *Liber de Coquina*, and a casserole similar to mac and cheese is recorded in a fourteenth century English cookbook. It was America's third president, the legendary gastronome Thomas Jefferson, who planted it firmly on these shores. Mac and cheese was fashionable when Jefferson lived in Paris following the Revolutionary War. According to Jack MacLaughlin in his book, *Jefferson and Monticello: The Biography of a Builder,* Jefferson commissioned an associate to bring back an extruding machine for him from Italy, and he also imported wheels of Parmesan via Marseilles during his presidency. Mac and cheese was served at a White House state dinner in 1802, and the dish was basically macaroni cooked until soft and then combined with butter and

Parmesan. The first American recipe appeared in Mary Randolph's *The Virginia Housewife* in 1824. While the roots of mac and cheese in America run as deep as those of a California redwood, only during the past few decades has the dish been truly admired by chefs as well as diners.

Part of the problem has been the ubiquitous blue box. Kraft introduced mac and cheese in 1937, in the middle of the Great Depression. It would feed a family of four for less than a quarter, and with rationing during World War II, it became a staple in many households.

Mac and cheese, unlike cheese fondue, never cycled out of fashion. It's just that people outgrew it when their adult teeth grew in and their adult tastes developed. Mothers today still know that, when all else fails, even finicky eaters will down a bowl of mac and cheese. I see this in action at my niece's house: the box of Annie's organic bunnies comes out when her three children have rejected all other foods. And these are children who love sushi and crave fresh fruit more than cookies! But there are times when the only boxed mac and cheese will satisfy.

Boxed mac and cheese also reinforced in Americans' minds that this was an inexpensive dish. While they were willing to pay $18 or $20 for pasta with cheese sauce at an Italian restaurant, mac and cheese, even if it wasn't neon orange, was supposed to be cheap.

We can thank New American chefs for changing that perception. In the same way that they list apple pandowdy instead of *tarte tatin* on their menus, they call it what it is—mac and cheese. They make it with artisanal cheeses, vegetables, herbs, seafood, and meats. In addition to seeing mac and cheese pop up on restaurant menus from coast to coast, in this century we've seen the birth of a small group of restaurants whose menus feature *only* mac and cheese.

Most of the recipes in this book are adapted from restaurants around the country. That means there is great variety in the formulation of the sauces, proportion of cheese to sauce, and topping. You'll find a wide range of creative recipes that have been tested to work as perfectly in your kitchen as they do in mine.

Chapter One

MAKING THE PERFECT MAC AND CHEESE

One of the reasons mac and cheese is popular is that it's so easy to make. If you know how to boil water, the dish is halfway finished. There's no fear of failure, like there is that your soufflé will fall like a leaden pancake or your *beurre blanc* will separate. Once you've made a white sauce you've mastered the key technique for making a world-class mac and cheese. Here's the secret to superior mac and cheese: Cook the pasta correctly, use a lot of high-quality cheese, and season it properly. It's that simple.

But don't discount pasta prowess: a perfectly done noodle is one of many subtle nuances that makes this simple food great. It was Auguste Escoffier, the famed French chef, who wrote, "The greatest dishes are very simple dishes." All cooking contains a bit of chemistry along with a large dollop of artistry. The focus of this chapter is to help you to understand the whys of the steps that go into mac and cheese–making.

Pasta Perfect

MAC AND CHEESE IS TRADITIONALLY MADE WITH DRIED PASTAS, and while the basic elbow macaroni, called *maccheroni* in Italian, remains the most popular, there are numerous shapes that work just as well. The recipes in this book adapted from restaurants specify the pasta they use, and the dishes I created draw from the same range of shapes.

Mac and cheese is best made with small, extruded shapes of dried pasta. While supple, fresh pastas are divine in other applications, they are not the best choices for mac and cheese. Part of mac and cheese is having a thick coating of sauce clinging to each individual piece of pasta, and fresh pasta collapses, rather than supporting the sauce. Shapes are easier to fork than rods or ribbons, and they trap the sauce on its journey to your mouth.

The best pastas have a high percentage of durum semolina, a high-gluten, exceptionally hard strain of wheat. Semolina refers to the milled texture, which is that of fine sand. The pasta should be a rich ivory rather than being snowy white in color.

As I collected recipes from chefs around the country, one name kept appearing as their choice—Barilla. When I did a test of pastas I found that Barilla was always excellent, especially the macaroni shape. However I also had great success with Ronzoni and DeCecco, both brands also recommended by a test panel at *Cook's Illustrated*. And in the category of *penne*, the noted food magazine chose Mueller's over all other brands.

There are some really expensive imported dried pasta at specialty food stores, and they're not worth the money. I've seen fancy shapes for $7 a pound or more, and they're no better than supermarket brands. Instead, put your money into the best cheeses you can afford.

Pasta Shapes

The small pasta shapes that work well for mac and cheese all cook to al dente in 6 to 10 minutes with thicker shapes taking slightly longer. That's a rule of thumb for how to choose one that will work. You don't want pasta that is longer than two inches. On the opposite page is a guide to shapes that are interchangeable when making mac and cheese.

The Elusive Al Dente

Al dente in Italian means "to the tooth" or "to the bite" and it refers to a texture that offers a bit of resistance when chewing. Al dente means firm but not hard. For vegetables the term frequently used to imply the same quality is crisp-tender.

When cooking pasta for mac and cheese the cooking time depends on how the dish is being presented. If the dish is baked in the oven after the pasta and sauce are joined, the pasta will continue to cook and it will become softer as it absorbs liquid from the sauce. For these dishes, the pasta should be a little too hard to be truly termed al dente. The pasta is then run under cold water to cool it down quickly so it doesn't continue to cook.

On the other hand, if the mac and cheese goes directly from saucing to serving, the pasta should be al dente. Always taste a piece of pasta about one minute earlier than the recommended cooking range to see how it's doing. If pasta is old it may take longer than a fresh box.

PASTA SHAPES

NAME (MEANING)	DESCRIPTION	COOKING TIME
ANELLI (Rings)	Medium, ridged tubes cut into thin rings	6-8 min.
CAMPANELLE (Bells)	Small flared cylinders	8-10 min.
CAVATAPPI (Corkscrews)	Short ridged pasta twisted into a spiral	8-10 min.
CAVATELLI (Little Plugs)	Tiny hot dog buns	6 to 8 min.
CONCHIGLIE (Shells)	Shells about 1 inch long	8-10 min.
DITALINI (Little Thimbles)	Very short round pieces	6-9 min.
FARFALLE (Butterflies)	Flat rectangles pinched in the center to form a bow	10-12 min.
FUSILLI (Twisted Spaghetti)	Long, spring-shaped strands	10-12 min.
GEMELLI (Twins)	Medium strands woven together and cut into 2-inch lengths	8-10 min.
MACCHERONI (Macaroni)	Thin, tubular pasta in various widths	8-10 min.
ORECCHIETTE (Ears)	Smooth, curved rounds about $1/2$ inch in diameter	6-9 min.
PENNE (Quills)	Small tubes with angle-cut ends	8-10 min.
RADIATORE (Radiators)	Short, thick, and ruffled	8-10 min.
ROTELLE (Wheels)	Spiral-shaped with spokes	8-10 min.
ROTINI (Spirals)	Two thick strands twisted	8-10 min.

ROTELLE

CONCHIGLIE

GEMELLI

CAVATAPPI

FARFALLE

PENNE

MACARONI

DITALINI

CAMPANELLE

ROTINI

Choices for Cheeses

THERE ARE A FEW CRITICAL FACTORS IN DETERMINING THE DIS- tinctive character of a cheese: the kind of milk used (cow, sheep, goat) and its fat content; the methods for cutting, cooking, and forming the curd; the type of culture; the salting process; and the ripening method. Cheeses do fall into families, usually determined by texture and occasionally by flavor.

The lists that follow are cheeses used frequently in mac and cheese. They are divided by firmness; however, you can make substitutions based on the flavor profile too.

SOFT CHEESES

These cheeses melt very easily when heated.

NAME	COUNTRY	BASE	FLAVOR
BOURSAULT	France	Cow	Mild to strong
BRIE	France	Cow	Mild to pungent
BRILLAT-SAVARIN	France	Cow	Mild, slightly sweet
BÛCHERON	France	Goat	Mild to mellow
CAMEMBERT	France	Cow	Mild to pungent
CROTTIN	France	Goat	Sharp
EXPLORATEUR	France	Cow	Very creamy, mild
LIMBURGER	Belgium	Cow	Strong, aromatic
MONTRACHET	France	Goat	Mild
SAINT ANDRÉ	France	Cow	Mild to tangy
VACHERIN	Switzerland	Cow	Mild to pungent

SEMI-SOFT CHEESES

These cheeses are firmer than soft cheeses, but they do not require a sharp knife for cutting.

NAME	COUNTRY	BASE	FLAVOR
AMERICAN	US	Cow	Mild
ASADERO	Mexico	Cow	Mild
ASIAGO	Italy	Cow	Piquant, sharp
BEL PAESE	Italy	Cow	Mild to robust
EDAM	Holland	Cow	Mild
FETA	Greece	Sheep	Salty, sharp
FONTINA	Italy	Cow	Mild and nutty
GOUDA	Holland	Cow	Mild, like Edam
HAVARTI	Denmark	Cow	Mild, frequently flavored
MANCHEGO	Spain	Sheep	Mild to mellow
MONTEREY JACK	US	Cow	Mild to mellow
MOZZARELLA	Italy	Cow	Mild and delicate
MUENSTER	Germany	Cow	Mild to mellow
PORT-SALUT	France	Cow	Mild to robust
RACLETTE	Switzerland	Cow	Full and fruity
TALEGGIO	Italy	Cow	Mild to Mellow

HARD CHEESES

Almost like wine, hard cheeses are aged in cellars for years. The more expensive cheeses tend to have been stored longer, creating a better quality cheese.

NAME	COUNTRY	BASE	FLAVOR
CHEDDAR	US	Cow	Mild to sharp
CHESHIRE	England	Cow	Mild to tangy
COLBY	US	Cow	Mild to mellow
EMMENTAL	Switzerland	Cow	Mild, sweet, nutty
GLOUCESTER	England	Cow	Slightly sharp
GRUYÈRE	Switzerland	Cow	Mild and sweet
JARLSBERG	Switzerland	Cow	Mild and sweet
KASSERI	Greece	Sheep	Sharp and piquant
LEICESTER	England	Cow	Mild to sharp
PARMESAN	Italy	Cow	Sharp and piquant
PROVOLONE	Italy	Cow	Bland acid flavor
ROMANO	Italy	Cow/goat	Sharp and piquant
SAPSAGO	Switzerland	Cow	Sharp and pungent
SWISS	US	Cow	Sweet, and nutty
TILLAMOOK	US	Cow	Mild to mellow

BLUE-VEINED CHEESES

These cheeses develop blue veins throughout from having been inoculated with starter bacteria.

NAME	COUNTRY	BASE	FLAVOR
BLEU DE BRESSE	France	Cow/goat	Piquant and peppery
DANISH BLUE	Denmark	Cow	Piquant and tangy
GORGONZOLA	Italy	Cow/goat	Piquant and peppery
MAYTAG BLUE	US	Cow	Piquant and tangy
ROQUEFORT	France	Sheep	Sharp and spicy
STILTON	England	Cow	Piquant and spicy

Buying and Storing Cheese

There's little question that mac and cheese made with good-quality cheeses is not an inexpensive dish. Imported cheeses are rarely less than $12 a pound, and easily run more than $20 per pound.

If you are lucky enough to live in an area with a real cheese shop where they cut the cheeses to order, you should flock to it. The cheeses will cost a little more per pound than those at the supermarket, and they will have been chosen by a knowledgeable person and cared for perfectly.

The next rung down is a high-quality grocer who has actual wheels of cheese in the case. The portion you buy might be wrapped in plastic, but it will have a stamp showing the packed-on date.

When you buy plastic-wrapped cheese, look at the wedge carefully. Cheese can have blue mold or green mold, but if cheese has a yellow or pink mold it's gone bad. Even if it's encased in plastic, see if there is any ammonia smell, and if so, avoid that piece.

Ideally, cheese is never suffocated in plastic for too long. The cheese will take on the flavor of the plastic wrapper, and cheeses need the correct balance of temperature, humidity, and air circulation.

Cheese shops will wrap your cheese in cheese paper, which is a cross between waxed paper and parchment paper. If you bring cheese home in plastic, rewrap it immediately in waxed paper.

Cheese should be stored in the bottom bin of your refrigerator. That's where it's the warmest and most humid.

Making a Superior Sauce

THE MOST COMMON SAUCE USED FOR NAPPING THE NOODLES IN mac and cheese dishes is a Mornay sauce, which falls under the béchamel category of classic French sauces. I know it sounds fancy, but béchamel is white sauce and Mornay is its first cousin. "Mornay" merely indicates that cheese is melted into to the cream sauce.

The Crucial Cooking of the Roux

The first step is melting butter, although occasionally you can come across a sauce that calls for a mixture of butter and oil or oil alone. Into the butter goes flour, and the cooking together of these two simple ingredients gets the fancy name of a *roux*. Making the roux, pronounced "ROO" as in kangaroo, is the only crucial step to a good sauce. The purpose of stirring the butter and the flour is to coat the protein molecules in the flour with fat. This creates a finished sauce that is silky in texture and does not contain any taste of raw flour, an unattractive mouth feel that I equate to library paste.

It's important that the roux be stirred constantly over low heat. As it cooks, you'll see tiny bubbles foaming, and the mixture will appear to have increased in volume. This usually only takes one minute, but depending on the stove's temperature and the thickness of the pan, it can take longer.

The classic proportion of butter and flour is in equal amounts, however this ratio is hardly cast in stone, or even Jell-O™. More flour creates a thicker sauce, which is sometimes advantageous if using milk rather than cream.

Dairy Product Duty

All of the Mornay sauce recipes in this book call for the dairy product to be heated before it is whisked into the roux. Heating milk and cream requires constant vigilance to avoid a dramatic spillover onto your stove in what seems to be a second. As dairy products heat, the water content begins to evaporate from the surface, thus concentrating the fats and proteins in a thick layer at the top. As this layer increases in depth, the water vapor below it can't escape, so it eventually pushes up the whole top layer—and you have a real mess to clean up as soon as the stove cools down. To prevent this, you've got to watch that pot and stir it on a regular basis. I tested an old wives' tale about leaving a wooden spoon in the pot to provide a conduit for the water vapor to escape. It worked about half the time, and the other half of the time I went through a wad of paper towels dabbing up hot milk.

One suggestion is to heat the dairy products in a tall pan. That way you have a few more seconds to stir it or remove it from the heat before Mount Vesuvius erupts on your stove.

The hot milk or cream should be whisked in slowly. Should lumps appear it means the liquid was added too quickly or the flame was too high under the pan. Vigorous whisking will remove the lumps.

Adding the Cheese

Once the sauce has simmered for a few minutes, it becomes thicker, and it's easier to add the cheese. The cheese should be added gradually while stirring. If too much cheese is added at a time, the temperature of the sauce will drop below a simmer, and the cheese may form a giant lump that is difficult to melt easily without scorching the sauce. Don't worry if your sauce gets small cheese lumps. They'll melt down.

SAUCES ARE PART OF WHAT DEFINED CLASSIC FRENCH COOKING of the nineteenth and most of the twentieth centuries. In the early nineteenth century, chef Antonin Carême published an extensive list of sauces, and then Escoffier consolidated them to basically five "mother sauces." They are sauce béchamel, the cream sauce that serves as the basis for most mac and cheese; sauce espagnole, which is a brown sauce made from veal stock; sauce velouté, a roux-thickened sauce based on stock; sauce hollandaise, an emulsion of egg yolks, butter, and lemon juice; and sauce tomate, the basic tomato sauce.

Changing the Form

There are two schools of mac and cheese—you either finish it on top of the stove, or you bake it in the oven. In either case the finished sauce is married to the pasta harmoniously. While the two can be used interchangeably, they are not identical in preparation or quantities. First of all, pasta destined for the oven is undercooked slightly to compensate for the time it will simmer in the sauce, while skillet versions are cooked to the proper al dente.

Then there is the amount of sauce required. If you want to transform a skillet dish into an oven version, increase the amount of sauce by one third. Oven-baked mac and cheese should look almost soupy when it goes into the oven. But the reverse is not true. If you want to transform a baked dish to one cooked entirely on the stove, use the same amount of cheese, but cut back on the amount of liquid by one fourth.

Individual Servings

Restaurants serve mac and cheese as individual portions, and so can you. At some restaurants they merely scoop an amount onto a plate or into a dish. But others have an array of serving pieces, from six-inch cast iron skillets to ceramic gratin pans, that they use for a more dramatic presentation.

Gratin dishes are low and flat. They take best to skillet versions that are then browned, either with a crunchy topping or a sprinkling of additional cheese, under the oven broiler.

An alternative for individual servings of oven-baked recipes is ovenproof onion soup bowls or eight-ounce ramekins. The changes in this case are the baking temperature and time. The small bowls should be baked at 400°F for 12 to 15 minutes, or until they are bubbly and the topping is brown. For a smaller amount of mac and cheese to go on a plate next to an entrée, use a muffin pan. Grease the cups of a 12-tin muffin pan heavily with vegetable oil spray, and sprinkle plain breadcrumbs on the inside. Use one of the oven-baked recipes, and fill the cups with the mixture, packing it down firmly. Sprinkle with whatever topping is suggested, and then bake them at 400°F for 10 to 12 minutes. Allow them to sit for 5 minutes, and then carefully take the mac and cheese muffins out of the cups with a spoon.

Crunchy Toppings

A CRUNCHY TOPPING IS PART OF THE JOY OF EATING A BAKED MAC and cheese. The dish emerges from the oven bubbling, and on top is a brown layer the color of a tan from a long Caribbean vacation. The macaroni and its sauce are smooth and soft, and then you get little bits of crunchy texture from the topping in each bite. Sometimes the topping is just additional cheese. Parmesan is commonly used in this way because it does harden so nicely. Each of the baked recipes in this book contains its own topping, but if you want to convert a stove-top recipe to an oven-baked one, as outlined in the section above, here are some alternate toppings. Pulse them in a food processor to evenly-sized crumbs, or seal them inside a plastic bag and smash them with a rolling pin.

- **PANKO BREADCRUMBS:** Until a few years ago, you'd have to look in the Asian food aisle of supermarkets to find these coarse Japanese crumbs used in traditional dishes like *tonkatsu*. But they've so grown in popularity that they're now found with all the other breadcrumbs, and most supermarket chains have inexpensive generic brands. Panko is made from bread that is baked by passing an electric current through the dough, which creates bread without crusts. Once ground, the flakes are airier, larger, and crisper than traditional breadcrumbs, and they are perfect for mac and cheese.

- **COMMERCIAL CRACKER CRUMBS:** In some parts of the country, buttery crackers such as Ritz are favorites, but you can use saltines or oyster crackers. While butter crackers have enough fat content on their own, other crackers should be mixed with a bit of melted butter so they will brown properly. Another option is cheese-flavored crackers such as Cheez-Its®.

- **SNACK FOODS:** Potato chips, tortilla chips, and fried onion rings are all candidates for mac and cheese topping. Make sure the flavors in the dish are harmonious with that of the topping. Barbecued potato chips, for example, would not work on a delicate dish.

THERE IS MUCH DEBATE AMONGST FOOD HISTORIANS ABOUT which *duc de Mornay* is the sauce's namesake. While a leading candidate is Philippe, duc de Mornay, a seventeenth century writer and diplomat, it would had to have been named for him posthumously because the sauce does not appear in the 1820 edition of *Le cuisinier royal,* which was the *Fannie Farmer* of its day for chefs of the aristocracy. We do know that sauce Mornay was on the menu in the nineteenth century at Le Grand Véfour, a legendary restaurant.

Advance Prep and Reheating Rules

ANY OF THE OVEN-BAKED RECIPES CAN BE PREPARED UP TO TWO days in advance and refrigerated without the topping. Keep the topping refrigerated separately, as it will absorb too much liquid from the sauce and will never get crispy.

If you do prepare the dish in advance, drizzle $\frac{1}{4}$ cup of heavy cream over the top, and stir it in lightly. Then cover the pan with foil and bake it at 375°F for 15 minutes. Then remove the foil, stir the casserole gently, and sprinkle on the topping. Bake it for an additional 20 to 25 minutes, or until it's bubbling.

For a skillet version, you can make the sauce up to two days in advance, but I suggest cooking the pasta right before you serve it. Pasta refrigerated by itself becomes gummy, and if the pasta is mixed with the sauce in advance it is difficult to reheat it without scorching. Make the sauce, and reheat it over low heat while the pasta cooks, and then join the two.

As you can imagine, I had a lot of leftover mac and cheese while developing the recipes for this book. Not since I wrote my ice cream book, *Scoop*, have I been so popular with my neighbors. When reheating mac and cheese, we found that those few dishes made without a roux did not reheat as well as those made with some flour. For reheating, low heat is the key, and adding additional milk helps, too.

In the conventional oven, reheat mac and cheese, covered with foil, at 325°F. The amount of time depends on the amount you're reheating. It's also possible to reheat it in the microwave. Add a bit of milk and cover the microwave-safe bowl with plastic wrap. Microwave on medium-low (40 percent power) and stir it often.

Gluten-Free Alteration

THERE ARE MILLIONS OF PEOPLE WHO NOW FOLLOW A GLUTEN-free diet. Gluten is a protein found in wheat, barley, and rye, so it's obviously part of traditional pastas. People with celiac disease or other related conditions have to avoid this protein, which means that pasta is out, as are thousands of baked goods, and many prepared foods that include gluten.

As awareness of gluten intolerance has grown, so have the options to improve the quality of life for those on a gluten-free diet. There are now many brands of gluten-free pastas on the market. Most of them are made with rice flour, although I've also seen some made from garbanzo bean flour or fava bean flour.

But that's only half the problem. The other half is the use of flour to make the roux for the sauce. I've written two cookbooks on gluten-free cooking, and after much experimentation, I've devised a formulation that solves this problem.

For each 2 tablespoons of all-purpose flour specified in a recipe use 2 tablespoons of rice flour and 2 teaspoons of cornstarch. Then follow the recipe for the Mornay sauce, using this substitution as a guide.

A Note about Serving Sizes

WITH THE EXCEPTION OF THE FINGER FOODS IN CHAPTER 2 AND THE desserts in Chapter 8, all of these recipes call for $^1/_2$ pound of pasta. This amount creates four servings that I would call luncheon-sized, and six that are side dishes. If you want to serve the mac and cheese as a more substantial entrée, these recipes will make three to four servings, depending on the appetites of the people to whom you're serving it.

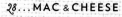

Chapter 2

FINGER FOODS

Cocktail party-quality hors d'oeuvres have taken off during the past decade, to everyone's delight. It's common today to be handed shot glasses of soups or spoons filled with tuna tartare. Mac and cheese can also join the ranks of finger food, as you'll discover when cooking the recipes in this chapter. Fried bits of mac and cheese have become popular in casual restaurants nationally, and they definitely qualify as finger foods, as do spring rolls. But there are a few baked options amongst these recipes too. It's important that the mac and cheese is either made into a hand-holdable item, or that it's supported by something strong enough to contain it.

Any recipe in the book can become a finger food if served in miniature phyllo shells, found in the freezer aisle at supermarkets. Or feel free to substitute another recipe for the ones given in this chapter to fill tortilla cups or spring rolls, or to top Parmesan crisps.

MAC AND CHEESE BITES

Adapted from The Boundary, Chicago IL

The Boundary has two locations in the Chicago area, and both are known for these fried mac and cheese bites. The sauce binding the bites gets some heat from the jalapeño Jack and complexity from the addition of Gorgonzola. They're delicious plain, or dipped in marinara sauce or even ranch dressing.

MAKES 3 DOZEN

$1/2$ pound ditalini

4 ounces Velveeta

$1/3$ cup vegetable stock

4 ounces jalapeño Jack, grated

2 tablespoons crumbled Gorgonzola

Salt and freshly ground black pepper to taste

2 cups panko breadcrumbs

3 tablespoons chopped fresh parsley

1 tablespoon fresh thyme (substitute $3/4$ teaspoon dried)

1 tablespoon chopped fresh rosemary (substitute 1 teaspoon dried)

1 garlic clove

3 tablespoons olive oil

All-purpose flour for dredging

3 large eggs

Line a rimmed baking sheet with parchment paper.

Bring a pot of salted water to a boil over high heat. Cook the pasta until it is al dente. Drain the pasta, run it under cold water, and refrigerate it in a mixing bowl.

Combine the Velveeta and stock in a saucepan over low heat. Cook, stirring frequently, until the mixture comes to a simmer. Add the cheese to the sauce by $1/2$-cup measures, stirring until the cheese melts before making another addition. Pour the sauce over the pasta, and stir well. Season to taste with salt and pepper, and transfer the pasta to the prepared pan. Pack it to an even thickness of $3/4$ inch. Freeze the pan for 3 to 4 hours, or until frozen solid.

While the macaroni freezes, prepare the crumb coating. Place the panko in a food processor fitted with the steel blade or in a blender. Process, using on-and-off pulsing, until the crumbs are half of their original size. Transfer the crumbs to a mixing bowl. Combine the parsley, thyme, rosemary, garlic, and oil in the processor or blender, and purée until smooth. Stir the herbs into the panko, and season to taste with salt and pepper. Set aside in a shallow bowl.

2 tablespoons whole milk
Vegetable oil for frying

Cut the frozen macaroni and cheese into 1-inch squares. Return the pan to the freezer for 30 minutes.

Place the flour in a shallow bowl. Combine the eggs and milk in another shallow bowl, and whisk well.

Coat the squares with the flour, shaking to remove any excess. Dip the squares in the egg wash, and then immediately into the crumb mixture. Pat the squares gently so that the crumbs adhere. Return the squares to the freezer until ready to cook.

Heat 1½ inches of vegetable oil in a deep-sided skillet or Dutch oven over high heat to a temperature of 350°F. Fry the pasta squares in the hot oil. Be careful to not crowd the pan. Cook for 3 to 4 minutes, turning them gently with a slotted spatula until browned on all sides. Drain well on paper towels, and serve immediately.

Note: The squares can be coated and frozen for up to 3 months. Wrap them tightly in plastic, then in a layer of foil.

BOTH VELVEETA AND AMERICAN CHEESE ARE LEGALLY TERMED "pasteurized processed cheese foods." Velveeta, now owned by Kraft, gained its name because it melted like velvet. It was introduced as a product in the 1920s, and because of its melting ability, it was used almost exclusively for mac and cheese until the 1960s. It's estimated that 5 percent of the population buys more than 75 percent of the Velveeta sold, so it obviously still has millions of fans.

ORZO ARANCINI

Arancini (pronounced ar-rahn-CHEE-neh), small fried balls of risotto, are one of my favorite hors d'oeuvres, and they're a great way to use up leftover risotto. That is, assuming there is leftover risotto. But I'd never make something so laborious just to have leftovers. Orzo, the versatile rice-shaped pasta, is far easier and quicker to make, and these balls are just as delicious.

MAKES 3 DOZEN

$^1/_2$ pound orzo

$^2/_3$ cup chicken stock

1 bay leaf

$^1/_4$ cup ($^1/_2$ stick) unsalted butter

1 large shallot, chopped

1 cup all-purpose flour, divided

$^1/_4$ cup dry white wine

$^1/_2$ cup heavy cream, warmed

1 tablespoon chopped fresh parsley

1 teaspoon fresh thyme (substitute $^1/_4$ teaspoon dried)

2 ounces freshly grated Parmesan

Salt and freshly ground black pepper to taste

4 large eggs, well beaten, divided

2 tablespoons whole milk

2 cups Italian breadcrumbs

Vegetable oil for frying

Bring a pot of salted water to a boil over high heat. Cook the pasta until it is past al dente and is soft. Drain the pasta and return it to the pot.

Place the chicken stock and bay leaf in a small saucepan and bring to a boil over high heat. Reduce to about $^1/_4$ cup. Discard the bay leaf and set the stock aside.

Heat the butter in a saucepan over medium heat. Add the shallot and cook, stirring frequently, for 3 minutes, or until the shallot is translucent. Stir in 3 tablespoons of the flour and cook, stirring constantly, for 1 minute, or until the mixture turns slightly beige, is bubbly, and appears to have grown in volume. Increase the heat to medium, and slowly whisk in the reduced stock, wine, and warm cream. Bring to a boil, whisking frequently. Reduce the heat to low, stir in the parsley and thyme, and simmer the sauce for 2 minutes. Add the cheese to the sauce by $^1/_2$-cup measures, stirring until the cheese melts before making another addition. Pour the sauce over the pasta, and stir well. Season to taste with salt and pepper. Place the pasta in a mixing bowl and chill well.

Stir 1 of the beaten eggs into the pasta mixture. Form the pasta into generous tablespoon-sized balls and set on a rimmed baking sheet lined with waxed paper.

Place the remaining flour in a shallow bowl. Combine (*continued*) the remaining eggs and milk in another shallow bowl, and whisk well. Place the bread-crumbs in a third bowl.

Coat the balls with the flour, shaking to remove any excess. Dip the balls in the egg wash, and then immediately into the breadcrumbs. Pat the balls gently so that the crumbs adhere. Return the balls to the refrigerator until ready to cook.

Heat 2 inches of vegetable oil in a deep-sided skillet or Dutch oven over high heat to a temperature of 350°F. Fry the pasta balls in the hot oil. Be careful to not crowd the pan. Cook for 2 to 3 minutes, turning them gently with a slotted spoon until browned on all sides. Drain well on paper towels, and serve immediately.

Note: The balls can be fried up to 2 days in advance and refrigerated, tightly covered. Reheat them in a 375°F oven for 4 to 6 minutes, or until hot.

Variations:

· Press $1/2$-inch cubes of mozzarella, Gruyère, Swiss, or Cheddar in the center of each ball.
· Add 3 ounces chopped prosciutto or salami to the pasta mixture.
· Add $1/2$ cup chopped cooked spinach to the pasta mixture.
· Substitute seafood stock for the chicken stock, and add 2 ounces chopped cooked shrimp, crabmeat, or lobster to the pasta.

THERE'S A REASON WHY BAY LEAVES SHOULD ALWAYS BE discarded. Although they add a pungent and woodsy flavor and aroma to dishes, they can be quite a bitter mouthful if you accidentally eat one. That's also why bay leaves are always added whole. If they were broken into pieces, it would be a real scavenger hunt to retrieve them.

MAC AND CHEESE SPRING ROLLS

Adapted from Cafeteria, New York, NY

During the past fourteen years Cafeteria, which is open around the clock, has become almost a landmark in the Chelsea section on the West Side of Manhattan. One of the signature dishes is Mac and Cheese Spring Rolls. The sauce, made with Cheddar and smoked Gouda, is also served as a dipping sauce on the side.

MAKES 8

$^1/_2$ pound macaroni

$^1/_4$ cup ($^1/_2$ stick) unsalted butter

3 tablespoons all-purpose flour

$1^1/_2$ cups whole milk, warmed

1 cup heavy cream, warmed

1 pound Cheddar, grated

$^1/_2$ pound smoked Gouda, grated

8 scallions, white parts and 4 inches of green tops, chopped, divided

Salt and freshly ground black pepper to taste

1 teaspoon granulated sugar

8 ($8^1/_2$-inch) spring roll wrappers (rice paper pancakes)

Vegetable oil spray

Vegetable oil for frying

Bring a pot of salted water to a boil over high heat. Cook the pasta until it is al dente. Drain the pasta, run it under cold water, and refrigerate it in a mixing bowl.

Heat the butter in a saucepan over medium-low heat. Stir in the flour and cook, stirring constantly, for 1 minute, or until the mixture turns slightly beige, is bubbly, and appears to have grown in volume. Increase the heat to medium, and slowly whisk in the warm milk and cream. Bring to a boil, whisking frequently. Reduce the heat to low, and simmer the sauce for 2 minutes. Add the cheese to the sauce by $^1/_2$-cup measures, stirring until the cheese melts before making another addition.

Set aside 1 cup of the sauce. Pour the remaining sauce over the pasta, add $^1/_2$ cup of the scallions, and stir well. Season to taste with salt and pepper. Chill well.

To form the spring rolls, fill a wide mixing bowl with very hot tap water, and stir in the sugar until it is dissolved. Place a damp tea towel in front of you on the counter. Place the rice paper pancakes on a plate, and cover with a barely damp paper towel. (You should fill one rice paper pancake at a time, keeping the remainder covered so they don't dry out.)

(continued)

Totally immerse the pancake in the hot water for 2 seconds. Remove it and place it on the damp tea towel; it will become pliable within a few seconds. Gently fold one third of the pancake towards the center. Place about 3 tablespoons of the chilled mac and cheese on the doubled-over edge and shape it into a log, leaving a 2-inch margin on each end of the log. Lightly spray the pancake with vegetable oil spray. Fold both sides in towards the center, as if rolling up a burrito, then roll the pancake tightly over the filling. Place the roll on the baking sheet, and continue to fill the rice paper pancakes in the same manner.

Heat 1½ inches of vegetable oil in a deep-sided skillet or Dutch oven over high heat to a temperature of 350°F. Reheat the reserved cheese sauce, stir in the remaining scallions, and season to taste with salt and pepper.

Place the spring rolls in the hot oil. Be careful to not crowd the pan. Cook for 4 to 5 minutes, turning them gently with a slotted spatula until they are browned on all sides. Drain well on paper towels, and serve immediately.

Note: The spring rolls can be prepared up to frying 2 days in advance and refrigerated, tightly covered.

THE KEYS TO PROPER FRYING ARE THE TEMPERATURE OF THE oil, and how much food is placed in the pan at the same time. A candy thermometer is the most accurate way to judge the temperature, but if you don't have one, drop a small cube of bread into the oil. If the oil bubbles furiously and the cube turns brown within 10 seconds, the oil is hot enough. Once at the correct heat, don't crowd the pan because cold food brings down the oil temperature quickly.

MAC AND CHEESE CARBONARA ON PARMESAN CRISPS

This dish really captures the potential of cooking with Parmesan cheese. The simple crisps are merely Parmesan baked with a few grains of flour until they turn into brown and crispy cookies. The flavor of the Parmesan emerges in a different fashion in the pasta made with bacon, egg, and lots of black pepper.

MAKES 2$\frac{1}{2}$ DOZEN

5 ounces freshly grated Parmesan, divided

3 tablespoons all-purpose flour

$\frac{1}{8}$ teaspoon cayenne

1 ounce bacon, diced

3 ounces ditalini

1 large egg, beaten

Salt and lots of freshly ground black pepper to taste

2 tablespoons chopped fresh parsley, for serving

Preheat the oven to 375°F. Line 2 baking sheets with silicone baking mats or parchment paper.

Reserve $\frac{1}{2}$ cup of the Parmesan. Combine the remaining Parmesan, flour, and cayenne in a mixing bowl. Place 1-tablespoon portions on the baking sheets, leaving 1$\frac{1}{2}$ inches between the mounds, tossing the cheese mixture frequently to keep the flour evenly distributed. Press the mounds flat with your fingers or the back of a spatula. Bake for 9 to 12 minutes, or until brown. Cool the crisps on the baking sheets for 2 minutes, then remove them with a spatula to a cooling rack to cool completely. These can be made up to a week ahead and kept in an airtight container at room temperature.

When you are ready to serve, cook the bacon in a skillet for 5 to 7 minutes, or until crisp. Remove the bacon from the skillet with a slotted spoon, and drain on paper towels. Reserve the bacon grease.

Bring a pot of salted water to a boil over high heat. Cook the pasta until it is al dente. Drain the pasta, reserving $\frac{1}{4}$ cup of the pasta cooking water.

Beat the egg with the reserved cheese and 2 tablespoons of the pasta cooking water. Add the pasta to the reserved skillet with the bacon grease, and cook over medium heat until the pasta is very hot.

Remove the skillet from the heat, and add the egg mixture. Stir until the sauce is creamy and the eggs are cooked. Return the skillet to very low heat if the mixture is runny and does not become thick, but be careful not to allow the egg to come to a boil or it will scramble. Add a bit more of the pasta water if the mixture is too thick. Stir in the bacon and season to taste with salt and lots of freshly ground black pepper.

To serve, place a scant tablespoon of the pasta on top of each crisp, and sprinkle with the parsley. Serve immediately.

Note: The crisps can be prepared up to 3 days in advance and kept at room temperature in an airtight container. Do not make the pasta until just before serving

THE BEST PLACE TO STORE EGGS IS IN THEIR CARDBOARD CARton. The carton helps prevent moisture loss, and shields the eggs from absorbing odors from other foods. If you're not sure if your eggs are fresh, submerge them in a bowl of cool water. If they stay on the bottom, they're fine. If they float to the top, it shows they're old: eggs develop an air pocket at one end as they age.

MINI-MAC CANAPÉS

Consider this recipe a formula rather than a singular dish. You can vary the cheeses, add herbs or spices, and personalize it in myriad ways. What makes these delectable two-bite canapés stick together is a very thick sauce and an egg yolk. My guests have adored mac and cheese as "finger food."

MAKES 18

2 tablespoons unsalted butter, divided

$1/4$ cup toasted breadcrumbs

$1/4$ pound ditalini

1 tablespoon all-purpose flour

$1/3$ cup whole milk, warmed

2 ounces sharp Cheddar, grated

2 ounces Gruyère, grated

1 large egg yolk

1 tablespoon heavy cream

1 teaspoon Dijon mustard

Salt and freshly ground black pepper to taste

Preheat the oven to 425°F. Coat mini-muffin pans with 1 tablespoon of the butter. Sprinkle the greased tins with the breadcrumbs. (If you are baking in batches, evenly distribute the butter and breadcrumbs.)

Bring a pot of salted water to a boil over high heat. Cook the pasta until it is just beginning to soften to the al dente stage. Drain the pasta, run it under cold water, and return it to the pot.

Heat the remaining butter in a small saucepan over medium-low heat. Stir in the flour and cook, stirring constantly, for 1 minute, or until the mixture turns slightly beige, is bubbly, and appears to have grown in volume. Increase the heat to medium, and slowly whisk in the warm milk. Bring to a boil, whisking frequently. Reduce the heat to low, and simmer the sauce for 2 minutes. Add the cheese to the sauce by $1/2$-cup measures, stirring until the cheese melts before making another addition. Pour the sauce over the pasta, and stir well.

Beat the egg yolk with the cream and mustard, and stir into the pasta. Season with salt and pepper, and press the mixture into the prepared tins. Bake for 10 to 12 minutes, or until the cheese sauce is bubbly and the tops are light brown. Allow to sit for 5 minutes, then serve.

Note: The canapés can be baked up to 2 days in advance and refrigerated, tightly covered. Reheat them in a 375°F for 7 to 10 minutes, or until hot.

MEXICAN MAC AND CHEESE TORTILLA CUPS

The sauce on this pasta is somewhat spicy and has all the wonderful flavors of a traditional *chile con queso*, but it's a lot easier to eat.

MAKES 2 DOZEN

Vegetable oil spray

3 (10-inch) flour tortillas

$^1/_4$ pound ditalini

2 tablespoons olive oil

1 shallot, chopped

2 garlic cloves, minced

1 jalapeño or serrano chile, seeds and ribs removed, and finely chopped

1 tablespoon chili powder

$^1/_2$ teaspoon ground cumin

$^1/_2$ teaspoon dried oregano, preferably Mexican

2 tablespoons unsalted butter

2 tablespoons all-purpose flour

$^3/_4$ cup whole milk, warmed

2 ounces jalapeño Jack, grated

2 ounces mild Cheddar, grated

Preheat the oven to 350°F. Coat 2 (12-cup) mini-muffin pans with vegetable oil spray.

Wrap the tortillas in plastic wrap, and microwave on high (100 percent power) for 20 to 25 seconds, or until pliable. Cut 8 circles from each tortilla with a 2$^1/_2$-inch round biscuit cutter. Press the tortilla circles into the muffin pans, and spray them with vegetable oil spray. Bake the cups for 7 to 10 minutes, or until crisp and browned. Remove the cups from the pan, and transfer them to a wire cooking rack to cool completely.

Bring a pot of salted water to a boil over high heat. Cook the pasta until it is al dente. Drain the pasta, run it under cold water, and return it to the pot.

Heat the oil in a small skillet over medium-high heat. Add the shallot, garlic, and chile, and cook, stirring frequently, for 4 to 5 minutes, or until the vegetables soften. Stir in the chili powder, cumin, and oregano, and cook for 30 seconds, stirring constantly. Set aside.

Heat the butter in a small saucepan over medium-low heat. Stir in the flour and cook, stirring constantly, for 1 minute, or until the mixture turns slightly beige, is bubbly, and appears to have grown in volume. Increase the heat to medium, and slowly whisk in the warm milk. Bring to a boil, whisking frequently.

Salt and freshly ground
black pepper to taste

3 tablespoons chopped
fresh cilantro, for
serving

Reduce the heat to low, stir in the vegetable mixture, and simmer the sauce for 2 minutes. Add the cheese to the sauce by $1/2$-cup measures, stirring until the cheese melts before making another addition.

Add the sauce to the pasta, and season to taste with salt and pepper. Cook over low heat until the pasta is hot and coated with the sauce. To serve, fill the tortilla cups with the mac and cheese, and sprinkle with the cilantro. Serve immediately.

Note: The baked tortilla cups keep at room temperature for up to a week in an airtight container. The sauce can be prepared up to 2 days in advance and refrigerated. Bring it to a simmer over low heat. Do not cook the pasta until just prior to serving.

Chapter 3

CLASSIC COMBINATIONS

All of these recipes are basic, beloved mac and cheeses. There are no vegetables or additions of seafood, and not even a few crumbles of bacon. This is where mac and cheese began. But while these recipes use only cheeses, they can hardly be considered basic.

The key to a luscious mac and cheese is to create complexity by combining a number of different cheeses rather than using just one. Some of these recipes list four or five different cheeses of various textures and potency.

Think of these recipes like a conductor leading an orchestra. There are roles to be played by each instrument to a lesser or greater extent. And what comes out is a wonderfully balanced symphony.

HERBED MAC AND CHEESE

Adapted from Farmstead & La Laiterie, Providence, RI

Matt and Kate Jennings opened Farmstead, a shop selling only cheeses from small producers around the world, in 2006. Two years later they opened La Laiterie, a bistro with a cheese-oriented menu, in an adjoining space. The mac and cheese quickly became the one dish that could never be cycled off the menu. The addition of a restrained amount of fresh herbs, as well as creamy Brie, to the traditional mix of Gruyère and Cheddar makes their version richer than most.

MAKES 4 TO 6 SERVINGS

$^1/_2$ pound penne

4 ounces Brie

3 ounces Gruyère, grated

3 ounces sharp white Cheddar, grated

$^1/_4$ cup ($^1/_2$ stick) unsalted butter, divided

2 tablespoons all-purpose flour

$^1/_2$ teaspoon chopped fresh rosemary (substitute $^1/_4$ teaspoon dried)

$^1/_2$ teaspoon chopped fresh sage (substitute $^1/_4$ teaspoon dried)

$^1/_2$ teaspoon fresh thyme (substitute a pinch dried)

$^1/_4$ teaspoon freshly grated nutmeg

(continued)

Preheat the oven to 375°F. Grease a 13 x 9-inch baking pan.

Bring a pot of salted water to a boil over high heat. Cook the pasta until it is just beginning to soften to the al dente stage. Drain the pasta, run it under cold water, and return it to the pot.

Scrape the white rind off the Brie, and chop it finely. Combine the Brie with the Gruyère and Cheddar, and set aside $^1/_2$ cup of the cheese mixture.

Heat 2 tablespoons of the butter in a saucepan over medium-low heat. Stir in the flour and cook, stirring constantly, for 1 minute, or until the mixture turns slightly beige, is bubbly, and appears to have grown in volume. Stir in the rosemary, sage, thyme, and nutmeg. Increase the heat to medium, and slowly whisk in the warm milk. Bring to a boil, whisking frequently. Reduce the heat to low, and simmer the sauce for 2 minutes.

Add the cheese to the sauce by $^1/_2$-cup measures, stirring until the cheese melts before making another addition. Pour the sauce over the pasta, and stir well. Season *(continued)*

2 cups whole milk, warmed

Salt and freshly ground white pepper to taste

¾ cup plain breadcrumbs

to taste with salt and pepper, and transfer the pasta to the prepared pan.

Heat the remaining butter in a small skillet over medium heat. Add the breadcrumbs, and cook for 2 minutes, or until the crumbs are golden brown. Combine the browned crumbs with the remaining cheese mixture, and sprinkle it over the top of the dish.

Bake the casserole for 20 minutes to 30 minutes, or until the cheese sauce is bubbly and the crumbs on the top are deep brown. Allow to sit for 5 minutes, then serve.

Note: To prepare the dish in advance or reheat it, follow the instructions on page 26.

VEGETABLE OIL SPRAY IS A WONDERFUL WAY TO KEEP FOODS like cheese from becoming permanently bonded to your pans, but it has a tendency to coat the counters too. Open your dishwasher, and place the pan to be coated on the open door before you spray it. That keeps the counters clean, and any excess spray washes away the next time you use the dishwasher.

DUMAC & CHEESE

Adapted from DuMont Restaurant, Brooklyn, NY

DuMont Restaurant has become a landmark in the Williamsburg section of Brooklyn. It is named for the bright green neon sign salvaged from what was a television production facility, transformed to a light and airy restaurant in 2001. The kitchen is under the command of Polo Dobkin, a graduate of the French Culinary Academy, and one of the dishes for which he is known is this fairly classic and delicious version of mac and cheese.

MAKES 4 TO 6 SERVINGS

½ pound radiatore or rotini

¼ cup (½ stick) unsalted butter

¼ cup all-purpose flour

1¼ cups heavy cream, warmed

1 cup whole milk, warmed

4 ounces Gruyère, grated, divided

4 ounces sharp white Cheddar, grated, divided

Salt and freshly ground black pepper to taste

3 tablespoons plain breadcrumbs

Preheat the oven to 375°F. Grease a 13 x 9-inch baking pan. Bring a pot of salted water to a boil over high heat. Cook the pasta until it is just beginning to soften to the al dente stage. Drain the pasta, run it under cold water, and return it to the pot.

Heat the butter in a saucepan over medium-low heat. Stir in the flour and cook, stirring constantly, for 1 minute, or until the mixture turns slightly beige, is bubbly, and appears to have grown in volume. Increase the heat to medium, and slowly whisk in the warm cream and milk. Bring to a boil, whisking frequently. Reduce the heat to low, and simmer the sauce for 2 minutes.

Reserve ¾ cup of both the Gruyère and Cheddar. Add the remaining cheese to the sauce by ½-cup measures, stirring until the cheese melts before making another addition.

Pour the sauce over the pasta, and stir well. Season to taste with salt and pepper, and transfer the pasta to the prepared pan. Mix the reserved cheeses and breadcrumbs together, and sprinkle it over the top of the dish.

Bake the casserole for 20 to 30 minutes, or until the cheese sauce is bubbly and the crumbs on the top are deep brown. Allow to sit for 5 minutes, then serve.

Note: To prepare the dish in advance or reheat it, follow the instructions on page 26.

CHEDDAR AND JACK MAC AND CHEESE

Adapted from T.W. Martin's Public House, Waupaka, WI

Waupaka is in the central part of Wisconsin, about ninety miles north of Madison, and the region boasts a chain of spring-fed lakes. T.W. Martin's Public House is located in a building constructed in 1868, and now listed on the National Register of Historic Places. The stone walls and roughly hewn beams create a perfect setting for a menu of casual pub fare, and the mac and cheese is a favorite with customers.

MAKES 4 TO 6 SERVINGS

$\frac{1}{2}$ pound penne

$\frac{1}{4}$ cup ($\frac{1}{2}$ stick) unsalted butter, divided

$\frac{1}{2}$ cup finely chopped onion

3 garlic cloves, minced

2 cups chicken stock

3 tablespoons all-purpose flour

$1\frac{1}{2}$ cups heavy cream, warmed

12 ounces sharp Cheddar, grated, divided

4 ounces Monterey Jack, grated, divided

Salt and freshly ground white pepper to taste

$\frac{3}{4}$ cup crushed Cheez-It® White Cheddar crackers

Preheat the oven to 375°F. Grease a 13 x 9-inch baking pan.

Bring a pot of salted water to a boil over high heat. Cook the pasta until it is just beginning to soften to the al dente stage. Drain the pasta, run it under cold water, and return it to the pot.

Melt 1 tablespoon of the butter in a small saucepan over medium-high heat. Add the onion and garlic, and cook, stirring frequently, for 3 minutes, or until the onion is translucent. Add the stock, bring to a boil over high heat, and cook until the stock is reduced by two thirds. Set aside.

Heat the remaining butter in a saucepan over medium-low heat. Stir in the flour and cook, stirring constantly, for 1 minute, or until the mixture turns slightly beige, is bubbly, and appears to have grown in volume. Increase the heat to medium, and slowly whisk in the reduced stock and warm cream. Bring to a boil, whisking frequently. Reduce the heat to low, and simmer the sauce for 2 minutes.

Reserve $\frac{3}{4}$ cup of the Cheddar and $\frac{1}{4}$ cup of the Monterey Jack. Add the remaining cheese to the sauce by $\frac{1}{2}$-cup measures, stirring until the cheese melts before making another addition. Pour the sauce over the pasta, and stir well. Season to taste with salt and pepper, and transfer the pasta to the prepared pan. Mix the reserved cheese with the cracker crumbs, and sprinkle it over the top of the dish.

Bake the casserole for 20 to 30 minutes, or until the cheese sauce is bubbly and the crumbs on the top are deep brown. Allow to sit for 5 minutes, then serve.

Note: To prepare the dish in advance or reheat it, follow the instructions on page 26.

BY FAR THE EASIEST WAY TO GRATE CHEESE IS WITH THE SHR-edding attachment of a food processor. It takes minutes to do a pound, and the cheese is so fine that it melts almost instantly when it hits the hot sauce. If you're using a box grater, spray it first with vegetable oil spray. It will be easier to use and easier to clean.

MAC AND CHEESE WITH MUSTARD SAGE TOPPING

Adapted from The Pullman, Glenwood Springs, CO

Mark Fischer and his wife, Lari Goode, have pulled together a menu of sophi-sticated versions of classic American bar food at this popular restaurant in a town 180 miles west of Denver, at the confluence of the Colorado and Roaring Fork rivers. The restaurant was selected by *Esquire* as one of the "Best New Restaurants of 2011," and the mac and cheese with its flavorful topping is one of their favorite dishes.

MAKES 4 TO 6
6 SERVINGS

3 tablespoons unsalted butter, divided

1 cup fresh breadcrumbs

1/2 cup chopped fresh parsley

1 tablespoon Dijon mustard

1 tablespoon chopped fresh sage (substitute 1 teaspoon dried)

1/2 pound macaroni

1 tablespoon all-purpose flour

2 cups heavy cream, warmed

Pinch of freshly grated nutmeg

1/4 teaspoon cayenne pepper

8 ounces Gruyère, grated

8 ounces aged white Cheddar, grated

Salt and freshly ground black pepper to taste

Preheat the oven to 400°F. Grease a 13 x 9-inch baking pan. Line a baking sheet with heavy-duty aluminum foil.

Melt 2 tablespoons of the butter in a microwave-safe bowl. Combine the butter, breadcrumbs, parsley, mustard, and sage in a mixing bowl, and mix well. Bake the crumbs on the baking sheet for 5 to 7 minutes, or until browned. Remove the pan from the oven, and set aside. Reduce the oven temperature to 375°F.

Bring a pot of salted water to a boil over high heat. Cook the pasta until it is just beginning to soften to the al dente stage. Drain the pasta, run it under cold water, and return it to the pot.

Heat the remaining 1 tablespoon of butter in a saucepan over medium-low heat. Stir in the flour and cook, stirring constantly, for 1 minute, or until the mixture turns slightly beige, is bubbly, and appears to have grown in volume. Increase the heat to medium, and slowly whisk in the warm cream. Bring to a boil, whisking frequently.

Reduce the heat to low, whisk in the nutmeg and cayenne, and simmer the sauce for 10 minutes, or until reduced by one third. Add the cheese to the sauce by 1/2-

cup measures, stirring until the cheese melts before making another addition. Pour the sauce over the pasta, and stir well. Season to taste with salt and pepper, and transfer the pasta to the prepared pan. Sprinkle the breadcrumbs over the top of the dish.

Bake the casserole for 20 to 30 minutes, or until the cheese sauce is bubbly and the crumbs on the top are deep brown. Allow to sit for 5 minutes, then serve.

Note: To prepare the casserole in advance or reheat it, follow the instructions on page 26.

I THINK SAGE IS ONE OF THE MOST UNDERUTILIZED HERBS. IN North America, we usually only use it in stuffing for the Thanksgiving turkey, and possibly for sausage, and in England it flavors sage Derby cheese. While it's used to a small extent in Italian cooking, it's virtually unknown in France. It has a slightly peppery flavor and a wonderful fresh aroma.

TRUFFLED MAC AND CHEESE

Adapted from Cafeteria, New York, NY

Fontina, with its nutty flavor and buttery texture, is the foil to aged sharp Cheddar in this mac, which is finished off with a healthy dose of aromatic truffle oil.

MAKES 4 TO 6 SERVINGS

$1/2$ pound macaroni

$1/4$ cup ($1/2$ stick) unsalted butter

2 tablespoons all-purpose flour

$1 1/2$ cups whole milk, warmed

1 cup heavy cream, warmed

1 pound aged Cheddar, grated, divided

$1/2$ pound fontina, grated, divided

2 tablespoons black truffle oil, divided

Pinch of cayenne pepper

Salt and freshly ground black pepper to taste

2 teaspoons chopped fresh chives, for serving

Preheat the oven to 375°F. Grease a 13 x 9-inch baking pan.

Bring a pot of salted water to a boil over high heat. Cook the pasta until it is just beginning to soften to the al dente stage. Drain the pasta, run it under cold water, and return it to the pot.

Heat the butter in a saucepan over medium-low heat. Stir in the flour and cook, stirring constantly, for 1 minute, or until the mixture turns slightly beige, is bubbly, and appears to have grown in volume. Increase the heat to medium, and slowly whisk in the milk and cream. Bring to a boil, whisking frequently. Reduce the heat to low, and simmer the sauce for 2 minutes.

Reserve $1/2$ cup of the Cheddar and $1/4$ cup of the fontina, and set aside. Add the remaining cheese to the sauce by $1/2$-cup measures, stirring until the cheese melts before making another addition. Stir in 1 tablespoon of the truffle oil and the cayenne. Pour the sauce over the pasta, and stir well. Season to taste with salt and pepper, and transfer the pasta to the prepared pan. Mix the reserved cheeses together, and sprinkle them over the top of the dish.

Bake the casserole for 20 to 30 minutes, or until the cheese sauce is bubbly and cheeses on the top are deep brown. Drizzle with the remaining truffle oil and sprinkle with the chives. Allow to sit for 5 minutes, then serve.

Note: To prepare the dish in advance or reheat it, follow the instructions on page 26.

MOLLY'S TRUFFLED MAC AND CHEESE

Adapted from Michael's on East, Sarasota, FL

Michael's on East put Sarasota on the dining map more than twenty-five years ago, and the restaurant was inducted into *Nation's Restaurant News's* Fine Dining Hall of Fame in 2009. Owner Michael Klauber named this dish after his daughter Molly.

MAKES 4 TO 6 SERVINGS

½ pound ziti

1 tablespoon unsalted butter

2 garlic cloves, minced

2½ cups heavy cream

2 tablespoons chopped fresh parsley

3 ounces Emmental, grated

3 ounces Gruyère, grated

3 ounces freshly grated Parmesan

3 tablespoons white truffle oil

Salt and freshly ground black pepper to taste

Bring a pot of salted water to a boil over high heat. Cook the pasta until it is al dente. Drain the pasta, run it under cold water, and return it to the pot.

Heat the butter in a saucepan over medium-low heat. Add the garlic and cook for 2 minutes, stirring frequently. Increase the heat to medium, and stir in the cream. Bring to a boil, whisking frequently. Reduce the heat to low, and simmer the sauce for 2 minutes.

Stir in the parsley, and add the cheese to the sauce by ½-cup measures, stirring until the cheese melts before making another addition. Add the sauce to the pasta, stir in the truffle oil, and season to taste with salt and pepper. Cook over low heat until the pasta is hot and coated with the sauce. Serve immediately.

Note: The sauce can be prepared without the addition of the truffle oil up to 2 days in advance and refrigerated. Bring it to a simmer over low heat. Do not cook the pasta until just prior to serving.

MOST TRUFFLE OIL IS NOT ACTUALLY MADE FROM TRUFFLES. It's a synthetic product that combines some of the organic aromas of truffles with olive oil or grapeseed oil. While some recipes call for white truffle oil and others call for black truffle oil, there's practically no difference in the aroma or flavor of the two, so because it's expensive, just get one.

SKILLET-FRIED CHEDDAR MAC AND CHEESE

Adapted from Zingerman's Roadhouse, Ann Arbor, MI

This mac and cheese was crowned the best in the country by Alton Brown on The Food Network, and it's one of the fastest to make because it's crisped in a skillet rather than in the oven. It was created by Alex Young, the chef at this full-service restaurant that opened in 2003. The skillet-frying caramelizes some of the cheese, a trick you can use for many mac and cheese dishes.

MAKES 4 TO 6 SERVINGS

- 1/2 pound macaroni
- 2 tablespoons unsalted butter
- 3 tablespoons chopped onion
- 1 bay leaf
- 1 tablespoon all-purpose flour
- 3/4 cup whole milk, warmed
- 2 tablespoons heavy cream, warmed
- 1/2 teaspoon Dijon mustard
- 8 ounces raw milk Cheddar, grated
- Salt and freshly ground black pepper to taste
- 1 tablespoon olive oil

Bring a pot of salted water to a boil over high heat. Cook the pasta until it is al dente. Drain the pasta, run it under cold water, and return it to the pot.

Heat the butter in a saucepan over medium-low heat. Add the onion and bay leaf, and cook, stirring frequently, for 3 to 5 minutes, or until the onion softens.

Stir in the flour and cook, stirring constantly, for 1 minute, or until the mixture turns slightly beige, is bubbly, and appears to have grown in volume. Increase the heat to medium, and slowly whisk in the warm milk and cream. Bring to a boil, whisking frequently. Reduce the heat to low, stir in the mustard, and simmer the sauce for 2 minutes.

Add the cheese to the sauce by 1/2-cup measures, stirring until the cheese melts before making another addition. Remove and discard the bay leaf. Pour the sauce over the pasta, and stir well. Season to taste with salt and pepper.

Heat a skillet over medium-high heat until it is very hot. Add the olive oil, swirling to coat. Add the macaroni, and allow it to cook for 3 minutes, or until a crust forms. Scrape the bottom of the crust with a metal spoon, and cook for another 3 minutes. Do not stir often. Cook until about 15 to 20 percent of the mixture is golden brown. Serve hot.

Note: The sauce can be prepared up to 2 days in advance and refrigerated. Bring it to a simmer over low heat. Cook and fry the pasta just prior to serving.

GOAT CHEESE AND BOURSIN MAC AND CHEESE

Adpated from Town Hall, Washington, D.C.

Paul Madrid, a California native, arrived in the nation's capital in 2000, and was hired at Paolo's, a famous Georgetown *boîte*, as a sous chef. Five years later, a group planning Town Hall, which many consider the *Cheers* bar of Washington, recruited him. The critically acclaimed food is far more sophisticated than one would expect to find at a friendly neighborhood watering hole. Chef Madrid's mac and cheese combines herbed Boursin and creamy goat cheese with a touch of white wine.

MAKES 4 TO 6 SERVINGS

- $^1/_2$ pound macaroni
- $^1/_4$ cup ($^1/_2$ stick) unsalted butter
- 3 tablespoons all-purpose flour
- $1^3/_4$ cups half-and-half, warmed
- $^3/_4$ cup heavy cream, warmed
- 3 tablespoons white wine
- $1^1/_2$ teaspoons Worcestershire sauce
- $^1/_2$ teaspoon hot sauce or to taste
- 8 ounces goat cheese, crumbled
- 2 ounces garlic and herb Boursin, crumbled
- Salt and freshly ground black pepper to taste
- 2 tablespoons chopped fresh parsley, for serving

Bring a pot of salted water to a boil over high heat. Cook the pasta until it is al dente. Drain the pasta, run it under cold water, and return it to the pot.

Heat the butter in a saucepan over medium-low heat. Stir in the flour and cook, stirring constantly, for 1 minute, or until the mixture turns slightly beige, is bubbly, and appears to have grown in volume. Increase the heat to medium, and slowly whisk in the warm half-and-half, warm cream, wine, Worcestershire sauce, and hot sauce. Bring to a boil, whisking frequently. Reduce the heat to low, and simmer the sauce for 2 minutes.

Add the cheese to the sauce by $^1/_2$-cup measures, stirring until the cheese melts before making another addition.

Add the sauce to the pasta, and season to taste with salt and pepper. Cook over low heat until the pasta is hot and coated with the sauce. Serve immediately, sprinkling parsley over each serving.

Note: The sauce can be prepared up to 2 days in advance and refrigerated. Bring it to a simmer over low heat. Do not cook the pasta until just prior to serving.

SHERRIED MAC AND CHEESE

Adapted from BRGR Kitchen + Bar, Kansas City, KS

This casual spot was selected by *Kansas City Magazine* **as the "Best New Rest-**aurant of 2010." It's headed up by Alan Gaylin, a noted restaurateur in the region. While the menu focuses on burgers, the mac and cheese has already become a signature item in the wood-paneled dining room.

MAKES 4 TO 6 SERVINGS

1/2 pound macaroni

3 tablespoons unsalted butter, divided

2 garlic cloves, minced

3 tablespoons dry sherry

1 cup whole milk

1/2 cup heavy cream

Pinch of freshly grated nutmeg

6 ounces Chihuahua cheese, grated

2 ounces freshly grated Parmesan

Salt and freshly ground white pepper to taste

1/2 cup fresh breadcrumbs

1 tablespoon chopped fresh parsley

1 tablespoon Boursin

Preheat the oven to 375°F. Grease a 13 x 9-inch baking pan.

Bring a pot of salted water to a boil over high heat. Cook the pasta until it is just beginning to soften to the al dente stage. Drain the pasta, run it under cold water, and return it to the pot.

Heat 2 tablespoons of the butter in a saucepan over medium-low heat. Add the garlic and cook, stirring frequently, for 1 minute. Increase the heat to medium, and whisk in the sherry, milk, and cream. Bring to a boil, whisking frequently. Reduce the heat to low, simmer the sauce for 2 minutes, and stir in the nutmeg.

Add the cheese to the sauce by 1/2-cup measures, stirring until the cheese melts before making another addition. Pour the sauce over the pasta, and stir well. Season to taste with salt and pepper, and transfer the pasta to the prepared pan. Melt the remaining butter, and mix it with the breadcrumbs, parsley, and Boursin. Sprinkle the mixture over the top of the dish.

Bake the casserole for 20 to 30 minutes, or until the cheese sauce is bubbly and the crumbs on the top are deep brown. Allow to sit for 5 minutes, then serve.

Note: To prepare the dish in advance or reheat it, follow the instructions on page 26.

MAC AND CHEESE PUDDING

Adapted from Ciro's, Sun Valley, ID

I met Mark Carraluzzi thirty years ago in Washington, D.C. where Mark was owner of The American Café, which was decades ahead of its time with its masterfully executed casual New American food. After a few more restaurants in the D.C. area, Mark and his wife Tracey moved to Sun Valley about five years ago, and now own Ciro's, popular both as a restaurant and for its adjoining market of take-out food and wine. This pudding, made with cottage cheese as well as Cheddar, cuts into squares almost like lasagna, and is creamy and delicious.

MAKES 4 TO 6 SERVINGS

$1/2$ pound macaroni

$1^3/4$ cups small curd cottage cheese

2 cups sour cream

3 large eggs

$1^1/4$ pounds sharp Cheddar, grated, divided

Salt and freshly ground black pepper to taste

3 tablespoons freshly grated Parmesan

Preheat the oven to 350°F. Grease a 13 x 9-inch baking pan.

Bring a pot of salted water to a boil over high heat. Cook the pasta until it is just beginning to soften to the al dente stage. Drain the pasta, run it under cold water, and return it to the pot.

Whisk the cottage cheese, sour cream, and eggs in a mixing bowl until smooth. Stir in all but $1^1/2$ cups of the Cheddar. Pour the sauce over the pasta, and stir well. Season to taste with salt and pepper, and transfer the pasta to the prepared pan. Combine the remaining Cheddar and the Parmesan, and sprinkle it over the top of the dish.

Bake the casserole for 40 to 50 minutes, or until the casserole is bubbly and the cheeses on the top are deep brown. Allow to sit for 5 minutes, then serve.

Note: To prepare the dish in advance or reheat it, follow the instructions on page 26.

VEGETABLE VERSIONS

When you think about classic Italian pasta dishes, numerous vegetarian ones spring to mind, and the addition of vegetables to mac and cheese is just as common. Whether simple or elaborate, with one vegetable or a whole cornucopia of ingredients, mac and cheese with veggies will pop with colors, textures and flavors. Adding vegetables to mac and cheese is also a sneaky way of getting more of them into what children are eating.

Not all vegetables work well, however. Beets turns the entire dish a blushing pink, and vegetables that are somewhat starchy, such as acorn or butternut squash, make the dish too filling, but it's easy to experiment and substitute one vegetable for another in these recipes as long as they belong to the same family. For example, many of these recipes include some spinach, but you could easily make them with Swiss chard, escarole, or broccoli rabe.

What's important is that the vegetables are cooked to the same al dente state as the pasta. Even though a baked mac and cheese gets bubbly before it emerges from the oven, the cooking time is not sufficient to soften hard foods like broccoli or asparagus. That's why all vegetables should be folded in fully cooked, especially if the dish is served from the stove and not baked.

Another reason to pre-cook the vegetables is so they won't give off liquid into the dish and take away from the creamy texture. Spinach, for example, gives off a tremendous amount of water, and this would surely dilute the sauce.

BIG KID MAC WITH SPINACH, CARAMELIZED ONIONS, AND TRUFFLE OIL

Adapted from Nosh, Dallas, TX

Avner Samuels, along with his fellow luminaries Dean Fearing and Robert Del Grande, put Texas on the map of culinary destinations back in the mid-1980s. Until Nosh, however, he was always cooking up fancy food at high prices. The menu at his new restaurant is as casual as its name, and Avner opened up a second Nosh in nearby Plano in 2011. His "Big Kid Mac" is truly that, with a number of fantastic cheeses and vegetables woven in, and a sprinkling of truffle oil on the top.

MAKES 4 TO 6 SERVINGS

$\frac{1}{2}$ cup (1 stick) unsalted butter, divided

1 tablespoon olive oil

1 medium onion, diced

$\frac{1}{2}$ teaspoon granulated sugar

Salt and freshly ground black pepper to taste

$\frac{1}{2}$ pound macaroni

2 large shallots, minced

2 garlic cloves, minced

$\frac{1}{3}$ cup all-purpose flour

1$\frac{1}{2}$ teaspoons smoked Spanish paprika

1 cup whole milk, warmed

$\frac{1}{2}$ cup heavy cream, warmed

2 ounces Port-Salut, diced

$\frac{1}{2}$ cup cream cheese, diced

(continued)

Heat 1 tablespoon of the butter and the oil in a small skillet over medium heat. Add the onion, sugar, salt, and pepper, and toss to coat the onions. Cover the skillet and cook for 5 minutes, stirring occasionally. Uncover the skillet, raise the heat to medium-high, and cook, stirring frequently, for 15 to 20 minutes, or until the onions are browned. Set aside.

Preheat the oven to 375°F. Grease a 13 x 9-inch baking pan.

Bring a pot of salted water to a boil over high heat. Cook the pasta until it is just beginning to soften to the al dente stage. Drain the pasta, run it under cold water, and return it to the pot.

Heat the remaining butter in a saucepan over medium-low heat. Add the shallots and garlic, and cook, stirring frequently, for 3 minutes, or until the shallots are translucent. Stir in the flour and cook, stirring constantly, for 3 minutes, or until the mixture turns golden brown, is bubbly, and appears to have grown in volume. Stir in the paprika, and cook for 30 seconds.

(continued)

2 ounces mild yellow
  Cheddar, grated

2 ounces Monterey Jack,
  grated

$1\frac{1}{2}$ ounces firmly packed
  shredded baby spinach

$\frac{1}{4}$ cup chopped fresh
  parsley

$\frac{3}{4}$ cup fresh breadcrumbs

1 to 2 tablespoons white
  truffle oil

Increase the heat to medium, and slowly whisk in the warm milk and cream. Bring to a boil, whisking frequently. Reduce the heat to low, and simmer the sauce for 2 minutes.

Add the Port-Salut, cream cheese, and Parmesan to the sauce by $\frac{1}{2}$-cup measures, and cook for 1 minute, or until the cheeses melt. Pour the sauce over the pasta. Add the caramelized onions, Cheddar, Monterey Jack, spinach, and parsley, and stir well. Season to taste with salt and pepper, and transfer the pasta to the prepared pan. Sprinkle the breadcrumbs on top of the dish.

Bake the casserole for 20 to 30 minutes, or until the cheese sauce is bubbly and the crumbs on the top are deep brown. Allow to sit for 5 minutes, then drizzle with the truffle oil, and serve hot.

Note: To prepare the dish in advance or reheat it, follow the instructions on page 26.

PORT-SALUT, OR PORT-DU-SALUT, IS MADE FROM PASTEURIZED cow's milk in Brittany. Trappist monks invented it during the nineteenth century, although it's now made in a creamery. The orange tone of the rind comes from annatto seed, and it's a semi-soft and mild cheese that melts easily into sauces.

MAC AND CHEESE WITH GORGONZOLA AND TOMATOES

The combination of sweet tomatoes, aromatic fresh basil, and earthy Gorgonzola cheese make this delicious dish complex and interesting. Serve it alongside any simple grilled or broiled entrée to elevate a mid-week meal into a holiday feast.

MAKES 4 TO 6 SERVINGS

½ pound macaroni

3 tablespoons unsalted butter

1 small onion, diced

2 garlic cloves, minced

3 tablespoons all-purpose flour

¼ cup dry white wine

2 tablespoons tomato paste

1 cup heavy cream, warmed

1 (14.5-ounce) can petite diced tomatoes, undrained

4 ounces whole-milk mozzarella, grated

2 ounces Gorgonzola, crumbled

Salt and freshly ground black pepper to taste

½ cup chopped fresh basil

½ cup freshly grated Parmesan

Bring a pot of salted water to a boil over high heat. Cook the pasta until it is al dente. Drain the pasta, run it under cold water, and return it to the pot.

Heat the butter in a saucepan over medium heat. Add the onion and garlic and cook, stirring frequently, for 5 to 6 minutes, or until the onion softens. Stir in the flour and cook over low heat, stirring constantly for 1 minute, or until the mixture turns slightly beige, is bubbly, and appears to have grown in volume.

Increase the heat to medium, slowly whisk in the wine and tomato paste, and whisk until smooth. Whisk in the warm cream and tomatoes. Bring to a boil, whisking frequently. Reduce the heat to low, and simmer the sauce for 2 minutes. Add the cheese to the sauce by ½-cup measures, stirring until the cheese melts before making another addition.

Add the sauce to the pasta, and season to taste with salt and pepper. Cook over low heat until the pasta is hot and coated with the sauce. Serve hot, sprinkling basil and Parmesan on each dish.

Note: The sauce can be prepared up to 2 days in advance and refrigerated. Bring it to a simmer over low heat. Do not cook the pasta until just prior to serving.

MAC AND CHEESE PRIMAVERA

Adapted from MacDaddy's Macaroni & Cheese Bar, Monroe, CT

MacDaddy's opened in 2011, and the owner, Robert Dunn, plans to turn this innovative concept into a franchise in the next few years. His chef, Kevin Larabee, comes up with concepts like this that join many colors and textures of vegetables.

MAKES 4 TO 6 SERVINGS

1/2 pound macaroni

1/4 cup (1/2 stick) unsalted butter

2 tablespoons all-purpose flour

2 cups whole milk, warmed

4 ounces fontina, grated

1/2 cup sliced cooked asparagus

1/4 cup frozen chopped spinach, thawed and drained

1/4 cup chopped cooked artichoke hearts

1/4 cup chopped sun-dried tomatoes packed in oil, drained

Salt and freshly ground black pepper to taste

Bring a pot of salted water to a boil over high heat. Cook the pasta until it is al dente. Drain the pasta, run it under cold water, and return it to the pot.

Heat the butter in a saucepan over medium-low heat. Stir in the flour and cook, stirring constantly, for 1 minute, or until the mixture turns slightly beige, is bubbly, and appears to have grown in volume. Increase the heat to medium, and slowly whisk in the warm milk. Bring to a boil, whisking frequently. Reduce the heat to low, and simmer the sauce for 2 minutes.

Add the cheese to the sauce by 1/2-cup measures, stirring until the cheese melts before making another addition. Stir the asparagus, spinach, artichoke hearts, and sun-dried tomatoes into the sauce. Add the sauce to the pasta, and season to taste with salt and pepper. Cook over low heat until the pasta is hot and coated with the sauce. Serve immediately.

Note: The sauce can be prepared up to 2 days in advance and refrigerated. Bring it to a simmer over low heat. Do not cook the pasta until just prior to serving.

THERE IS A VARIETY OF VEGGIES ADDED TO THIS DISH, AND THE only one that's really essential to the flavor is the sun-dried tomatoes. For the spinach and artichoke hearts, my suggestion is to shop the salad bar at the supermarket rather than ending up with lots of leftovers. And you can always substitute leftover green beans or any other vegetable for the asparagus.

MEDITERRANEAN MAC AND CHEESE WITH OLIVES

Adapted from S'MAC, New York, NY

S'MAC is short for Sarita's Macaroni. Sarita Ekya and her husband, Caesar, opened this trend-setting mac and cheese shop in 2006. Located in the East Village section of New York, the site is a full restaurant with beer and wine, as well as mac and cheese portions in various sizes, so it's possible to sample many of the dishes in one visit.

MAKES 4 TO 6 SERVINGS

8 garlic cloves, unpeeled

2 tablespoons olive oil, divided

6 ounces baby spinach

$\frac{1}{2}$ pound macaroni

2 tablespoons unsalted butter

2 tablespoons all-purpose flour

$1\frac{1}{2}$ cups whole milk, warmed

2 teaspoons chopped fresh thyme (substitute $\frac{1}{3}$ teaspoon dried)

1 teaspoon grated lemon zest

6 ounces goat cheese, crumbled

2 ounces Muenster, grated

$\frac{1}{4}$ cup pitted kalamata olives, diced

Preheat the oven to 375°F. Grease a 13 x 9-inch baking pan.

Toss the garlic cloves with 1 tablespoon of the oil on a piece of heavy-duty aluminum foil, and enclose the garlic in the foil. Place the packet on a baking sheet, and bake the garlic for 15 to 20 minutes, or until the cloves are soft. Remove the garlic from the oven, and when cool enough to handle, pop the cloves from their skins, and mash the garlic and oil into a paste. Set aside.

While the garlic bakes, heat the remaining oil in a skillet over medium-high heat. Add the spinach by the handful, letting each batch wilt before adding more. Remove the spinach from the skillet with a slotted spoon, and set aside.

Bring a pot of salted water to a boil over high heat. Cook the pasta until it is just beginning to soften to the al dente stage. Drain the pasta, run it under cold water, and return it to the pot.

Heat the butter in a saucepan over medium-low heat. Stir in the flour and cook, stirring constantly, for 1 minute, or until the mixture turns slightly beige, is bubbly, and appears to have grown in volume. Increase the heat to

Salt and freshly ground
black pepper to taste

3 ounces provolone, grated

$\frac{1}{4}$ cup plain breadcrumbs

medium, and slowly whisk in the warm milk. Bring to a boil, whisking frequently. Reduce the heat to low, stir in the thyme and lemon zest, and simmer the sauce for 2 minutes.

Add the cheese to the sauce by $\frac{1}{2}$-cup measures, stirring until the cheese melts before making another addition. Add the garlic paste, spinach and olives to the pasta. Pour the sauce over the pasta, and stir well. Season to taste with salt and pepper, and transfer the pasta to the prepared pan. Combine the provolone and breadcrumbs, and sprinkle the mixture over the top of the dish.

Bake the casserole for 20 to 30 minutes, or until the cheese sauce is bubbly and the crumbs on the top are deep brown. Allow to sit for 5 minutes, then serve.

Note: To prepare the dish in advance or reheat it, follow the instructions on page 26.

SPINACH, EVEN BABY SPINACH, CAN HAVE A LOT OF GRIT HIDDEN in the curls of its leaves. The best way to clean it is in a large bowl of cold water, rather than under cold running water. Soak the spinach, rubbing it with your hands to dislodge any dirt, then lift it from the bowl. Do not pour the spinach into a colander because the dirt will go right back onto the leaves.

SPINACH AND ARTICHOKE MAC AND CHEESE

Adapted from Elbows Mac n' Cheese, Cerritos, CA

Located in the southeastern portion of Los Angeles County, Cerritos is a residential community of about fifty thousand people. Punita Patel opened Elbows in 2010, and the kitchen is overseen by chef Leesadie Lands, a graduate of the California School of Culinary Arts.

MAKES 4 TO 6 SERVINGS

3 cups whole milk

1 small onion, halved

2 bay leaves

3 whole black peppercorns

1 clove

1/2 pound macaroni

1/4 cup (1/2 stick) unsalted butter

1/3 cup all-purpose flour

5 ounces freshly grated Parmesan, divided

5 ounces whole-milk mozzarella, grated, divided

2 ounces cream cheese, diced

Pinch of freshly grated nutmeg

1/2 cup frozen chopped spinach, thawed and drained

1/2 cup cooked artichoke hearts

Bring the milk to a simmer over medium heat, stirring frequently to prevent it from boiling over. Add the onion, bay leaves, peppercorns, and clove to the milk. Allow the milk to steep for 30 minutes. Strain the milk, and discard the solids.

While the milk steeps, preheat the oven to 375°F. Grease a 13 x 9-inch baking pan.

Bring a pot of salted water to a boil over high heat. Cook the pasta until it is just beginning to soften to the al dente stage. Drain the pasta, run it under cold water, and return it to the pot.

Heat the butter in a saucepan over medium-low heat. Stir in the flour and cook, stirring constantly, for 1 minute, or until the mixture turns slightly beige, is bubbly, and appears to have grown in volume. Increase the heat to medium, and slowly whisk in the strained warm milk. Bring to a boil, whisking frequently. Reduce the heat to low, and simmer the sauce for 2 minutes.

Reserve 3/4 cup of the Parmesan and 3/4 cup of the mozzarella. Add the remaining cheeses to the sauce by 1/2-cup measures, stirring until the cheese melts before making another addition. Stir in the nutmeg.

Salt and freshly ground
black pepper to taste

3/4 cup panko breadcrumbs

2 tablespoons chopped
fresh parsley

1 small garlic clove, minced

2 tablespoons olive oil

Pour the sauce over the pasta, add the spinach and artichokes, and stir well. Season to taste with salt and pepper, and transfer the pasta to the prepared pan.

Combine the breadcrumbs, parsley, garlic, and olive oil in a small bowl. Season to taste with salt and pepper. Sprinkle the remaining cheeses over the top of the dish, and then sprinkle with the breadcrumbs.

Bake the casserole for 20 to 30 minutes, or until the cheese sauce is bubbly and the crumbs on the top are deep brown. Allow to sit for 5 minutes, then serve.

Note: To prepare the dish in advance or reheat it, follow the instructions on page 26.

ARTICHOKES ARE PERENNIAL PLANTS THAT ARE PART OF THE thistle group of the sunflower family. Native to the Mediterranean, these plants are about six feet wide and four feet high when mature. What we actually eat is the flower bud, which would produce a wonderfully deep violet flower if not picked.

DILLED MAC AND CHEESE WITH GARLICKY SPINACH

I've always adored the way savory Greek dishes include some aromatic cinnamon to tempt the taste buds, and that is true of this dish. While the Mornay sauce is made with Spanish Manchego cheese, the garlicky spinach and fresh dill folded into it are Greek elements.

MAKES 4 TO 6 SERVINGS

$\frac{1}{2}$ pound macaroni

$\frac{1}{2}$ cup (1 stick) unsalted butter, divided

$\frac{1}{4}$ cup all-purpose flour

$2\frac{1}{2}$ cups whole milk, warmed

12 ounces Manchego, grated

$\frac{1}{2}$ teaspoon ground cinnamon

Pinch of freshly grated nutmeg

2 tablespoons olive oil

1 small onion, diced

4 garlic cloves, minced

1 pound baby spinach

$\frac{1}{2}$ cup minced fresh dill

Salt and freshly ground black pepper to taste

$\frac{1}{2}$ cup toasted plain breadcrumbs

6 ounces feta, crumbled

Preheat the oven to 375°F. Grease a 13 x 9-inch baking pan.

Bring a pot of salted water to a boil over high heat. Cook the pasta until it is just beginning to soften to the al dente stage. Drain the pasta, run it under cold water, and return it to the pot.

Heat 6 tablespoons of the butter in a saucepan over medium-low heat. Stir in the flour and cook, stirring constantly, for 1 minute, or until the mixture turns slightly beige, is bubbly, and appears to have grown in volume. Increase the heat to medium, and slowly whisk in the warm milk. Bring to a boil, whisking frequently. Reduce the heat to low, and simmer the sauce for 2 minutes. Add the cheese to the sauce by $\frac{1}{2}$-cup measures, stirring until the cheese melts before making another addition. Stir in the cinnamon and nutmeg.

Heat the oil in large skillet over medium heat. Add the onion and garlic, and cook, stirring frequently, for 4 to 6 minutes, or until the onion softens. Increase the heat to medium-high, and add the spinach by the handful, letting each batch wilt before adding more. Remove the spinach from the pan with a slotted spoon.

Stir the spinach mixture and dill into the sauce, then pour the sauce over the pasta, and stir well. Season to taste with salt and pepper, and transfer the pasta to the prepared pan.

Melt the remaining butter over medium heat. Add the breadcrumbs, and stir well. Toss the breadcrumbs with the feta to combine. Sprinkle the mixture over the top of the dish.

Bake the casserole for 20 to 30 minutes, or until the cheese sauce is bubbly and the crumbs on the top are deep brown. Allow to sit for 5 minutes, then serve.

Note: To prepare the dish in advance or reheat it, follow the instructions on page 26.

YOU CAN RINSE BUNCHES OF PARSLEY, CILANTRO, AND DILL, trim off the stems, and then wrap small bundles and freeze them. When you need some, you can "chop" it with the blunt side of a knife. It will chop easily when frozen, and this method produces far better flavor than dried.

MAC AND CHEESE MARGHERITA

Here's a mac and cheese version of one of my favorite pizzas, which I frequently serve for a crowd as a side dish. The tomatoes are oven-roasted which intensifies their innate sweetness, and the fresh basil sprinkled on before serving adds brightness to the mellow flavors.

MAKES 4 TO 6 SERVINGS

$1^{1}/_{2}$ pounds ripe plum tomatoes, halved, cored, and seeded

$^{1}/_{4}$ cup olive oil, divided

3 garlic cloves, minced

2 teaspoons fresh thyme (substitute $^{1}/_{2}$ teaspoon dried)

2 teaspoons granulated sugar

Salt and freshly ground black pepper to taste

$^{1}/_{2}$ pound cavatelli

$^{1}/_{4}$ cup ($^{1}/_{2}$ stick) unsalted butter

2 large shallots, minced

2 tablespoons all-purpose flour

$^{1}/_{2}$ teaspoon dried oregano

2 cups whole milk, warmed

7 ounces whole-milk mozzarella, grated

2 ounces freshly grated Parmesan, divided

(continued)

Preheat the oven to 425°F. Line a baking sheet with heavy-duty aluminum foil, and place a wire rack over the foil. Arrange the tomatoes on the rack, cut side up. Drizzle them with 2 tablespoons of the olive oil, and then sprinkle them with the garlic, thyme, sugar, salt, and pepper. Roast the tomatoes for 20 to 25 minutes, or until the tomatoes are shriveled. When cool enough to handle, remove and discard the peels, and coarsely chop the tomatoes. Set aside.

Reduce the oven temperature to 375°F. Grease a 13 x 9-inch baking pan.

Heat the butter in a saucepan over medium-low heat. Add the shallots and cook, stirring frequently, for 3 minutes, or until the shallots soften. Stir in the flour and oregano, and cook, stirring constantly, for 1 minute, or until the mixture turns slightly beige, is bubbly, and appears to have grown in volume. Increase the heat to medium, and slowly whisk in the warm milk. Bring to a boil, whisking frequently. Reduce the heat to low, and simmer the sauce for 2 minutes.

Add the mozzarella and $^{1}/_{2}$ cup of the Parmesan to the sauce by $^{1}/_{2}$-cup measures, stirring until the cheese melts before making another addition. Pour the sauce over the pasta, and stir well.

(continued)

½ cup firmly packed
  chopped fresh basil
½ cup plain breadcrumbs

Gently fold in the tomatoes and basil, season to taste with salt and pepper, and transfer the pasta to the prepared pan. Mix the remaining olive oil, remaining Parmesan, and breadcrumbs together, and sprinkle it over the top of the dish.

Bake the casserole for 20 to 30 minutes, or until the cheese sauce is bubbly and the crumbs on the top are deep brown. Allow to sit for 5 minutes, then serve.

Note: To prepare the dish in advance or reheat it, follow the instructions on page 26.

ANY ITALIAN DISH REFERRED TO AS *MARGHERITA* INCLUDES tomatoes, mozzarella, and basil, the colors of the Italian flag. But the identity of the queen for whom these dishes are famous is in dispute. Some food historians maintain that pizza Margherita was created in 1889 for the queen who was the wife of Alfonse of Aragón. But then there's another Queen Margherita who married to Italian King Umberto I. Regardless of the lady, the dish was created in Naples, although the combination of flavors now translates to many forms of food.

WILD MUSHROOM MAC AND CHEESE

Adapted from Chamberlain's Steak & Chop House, Dallas, TX

Chamberlain's has been heralded as one of the best in Dallas, and it is now one of a pair of restaurants owned by Richard Chamberlain, a trailblazer of New American cuisine. Lan Nickens is now in charge of day-to-day operations, and the Wild Mushroom Mac and Cheese is a dish for which the restaurant has become known.

MAKES 4 TO 6 SERVINGS

$^1\!/_2$ pound small penne

4 ounces fresh shiitake mushrooms, stemmed and sliced

4 ounces fresh oyster mushrooms, sliced if large

4 ounces cremini mushrooms, diced

$^2\!/_3$ cup olive oil, divided

1 shallot, chopped

1 garlic clove, minced

1 tablespoon chopped fresh parsley

2 teaspoons chopped fresh oregano (substitute $^2\!/_3$ teaspoon dried)

1 teaspoon fresh thyme (substitute pinch of dried)

3 cups heavy cream

4 ounces smoked Gouda, grated

2 teaspoons white truffle oil

Salt and freshly ground black pepper to taste

Preheat the oven to 350°F. Line a baking sheet with heavy-duty aluminum foil.

Bring a pot of salted water to a boil over high heat. Cook the pasta until it is al dente. Drain the pasta, run it under cold water, and return it to the pot.

Combine the shiitake mushrooms, oyster mushrooms, and cremini mushrooms on the baking sheet, and toss with $^1\!/_2$ cup of the olive oil. Roast the mushrooms for 8 to 10 minutes, or until lightly browned.

Heat the remaining oil in a deep skillet over medium-high heat. Add the shallot and garlic, and cook, stirring frequently, for 3 minutes, or until the shallot is translucent. Add the mushrooms, parsley, oregano, and thyme. Cook, stirring frequently, for an additional 3 minutes. Stir in the cream, and bring to boil over medium heat, stirring occasionally. Cook for 5 to 7 minutes over low heat, or until the liquid is reduced by one quarter. Add the cheese to the sauce by $^1\!/_2$-cup measures, stirring until the cheese melts before making another addition.

Add the pasta to the sauce, and cook until the pasta is heated through. Stir in the truffle oil and season to taste with salt and pepper. Serve immediately.

Note: The sauce can be prepared up to 2 days in advance and refrigerated. Bring it to a simmer over low heat. Do not cook the pasta until just prior to serving.

PARISIAN MAC AND CHEESE WITH SHIITAKE MUSHROOMS AND FIGS

Adapted from S'MAC, New York, NY

The combination of sweet dried figs with woody wild mushrooms and creamy Brie and Muenster cheeses make this an unusual, delicious dish. I served it on Thanksgiving last year as an alternative side dish to the usual suspects, and it was a huge hit.

MAKES 4 TO 6 SERVINGS

2 ounces dried figs, stemmed and diced

2 tablespoons olive oil, divided

$\frac{1}{2}$ pound macaroni

4 ounces Brie

$\frac{1}{4}$ cup ($\frac{1}{2}$ stick) unsalted butter, divided

4 ounces fresh shiitake mushrooms, stemmed and sliced

2 tablespoons all-purpose flour

$1\frac{1}{2}$ cups whole milk, warmed

2 ounces Muenster, grated

2 ounces Pecorino Romano, grated

2 tablespoons chopped fresh rosemary (substitute 2 teaspoons dried)

Preheat the oven to 375°F. Grease a 13 x 9-inch baking pan. Combine the figs and 1 tablespoon of the olive oil on a sheet of aluminum foil, and bake, uncovered, for 3 minutes. Set aside.

Bring a pot of salted water to a boil over high heat. Cook the pasta until it is just beginning to soften to the al dente stage. Drain the pasta, run it under cold water, and return it to the pot.

Scrape the white rind off the Brie, and chop it finely. Set aside. Heat 2 tablespoons of the butter and the remaining oil in a skillet over medium-high heat. Add the mushrooms and cook, stirring frequently, for 4 to 6 minutes, or until browned.

Heat the remaining butter in a saucepan over medium-low heat. Stir in the flour and cook, stirring constantly, for 1 minute, or until the mixture turns slightly beige, is bubbly, and appears to have grown in volume. Increase the heat to medium, and slowly whisk in the warm milk. Bring to a boil, whisking frequently. Reduce the heat to low and simmer the sauce for 2 minutes.

Add the cheeses to the sauce by $\frac{1}{2}$-cup measures, stirring until the cheese melts before making another addition.

Salt and freshly ground
black pepper to taste

3 ounces provolone, grated

$\frac{1}{4}$ cup plain breadcrumbs

Add the figs, sautéed mushrooms, and rosemary to the pasta. Pour the sauce over the pasta, and stir well. Season to taste with salt and pepper, and transfer the pasta to the prepared pan. Combine the provolone and breadcrumbs, and sprinkle the mixture over the top of the dish.

Bake the casserole for 20 to 30 minutes, or until the cheese sauce is bubbly and the crumbs on the top are deep brown. Allow to sit for 5 minutes, then serve.

Note: To prepare the dish in advance or reheat it, follow the instructions on page 26.

ALTHOUGH THE FRESH SHIITAKE MUSHROOM IS A RELATIVE newcomer to the American produce section, it is the granddaddy of all cultivated mushrooms. The Japanese have been cultivating them for more than 2,000 years. The ancient Greeks and Romans did not cultivate mushrooms; contrary to popular belief, they merely encouraged wild ones to grow. It was not until the eighteenth century, when Olivier de Serres was agronomist to French King Louis XIV, that mushroom cultivation began in Europe.

SWEET ONION MAC AND CHEESE

Adapted from The Coterie Room, Seattle, WA

Chefs Brian McCracken and Dana Tough have become a real force in the innovative dining scene in Seattle. The Coterie Room, which opened in 2011, was the fourth restaurant the duo launched in three years. Their mac and cheese has its foundation in *soubise*, a classic French sauce of creamy onions, which is then blended with a trio of cheeses and topped with a sprinkling of crispy fried shallots.

MAKES 4 TO 6 SERVINGS

$1/2$ pound orecchiette

1 tablespoon olive oil

1 cup canola oil, divided

$1/2$ cup (1 stick) unsalted butter, divided

1 large sweet onion, such as Vidalia or Maui, diced

Salt and freshly ground black pepper to taste

$1/3$ cup all-purpose flour

2 cups whole milk, warmed

2 ounces fontina, grated

3 tablespoons freshly grated Parmesan

2 ounces sharp white Cheddar, grated

1 large shallot, thinly sliced

$1/4$ cup rice flour (substitute cornstarch)

1 teaspoon snipped fresh chives

1 teaspoon chopped fresh parsley

Bring a pot of salted water to a boil over high heat. Cook the pasta until al dente. Drain the pasta, run it under cold water, and return it to the pot. Toss the pasta with the olive oil.

Heat 1 tablespoon of the canola oil and 2 tablespoons of the butter in a skillet over medium heat. Add the onion, and toss to coat with the fat. Reduce the heat to low, cover the pan, and cook the onion for 5 minutes. Raise the heat to medium-high, sprinkle the onion with salt and pepper, and cook, uncovered, for 7 to 10 minutes, or until the onion is golden brown. Puree the onion in a food processor fitted with the steel blade or in a blender, and set aside.

Heat the remaining butter in a saucepan over low heat. Stir in the flour and cook, stirring constantly, for 2 minutes, or until the mixture turns slightly beige, is bubbly, and appears to have grown in volume. Increase the heat to medium, and slowly whisk in the warm milk. Bring to a boil, whisking frequently. Reduce the heat to low, and simmer the sauce, stirring occasionally, for 10 minutes, or until it thickens.

(continued)

Add the cheese to the sauce by $\frac{1}{2}$-cup measures, stirring until the cheese melts before making another addition. Stir in the onion puree, and season the sauce to taste with salt and pepper.

While the sauce simmers, heat the remaining canola oil in a small saucepan to a temperature of 350°F. Coat the shallot slices with the rice flour, shaking off any excess. Fry the shallot slices for 1 to 2 minutes, or until golden brown. Remove the shallots from the oil with a slotted spoon, and drain on paper towels.

To serve, stir the sauce, chives, and parsley into the pasta. Cook over low heat until the pasta is hot and coated with the sauce. Serve immediately, garnishing each serving with some of the fried shallots.

Note: The sauce can be prepared up to 2 days in advance and refrigerated. Bring it to a simmer over low heat. The pasta should not be cooked and the shallots should not be fried until just prior to serving.

THE SUGAR CONTENT OF SWEET ONIONS SUCH AS VIDALIA, Bermuda, and Spanish is far higher than that of a normal onion, which is why they're always the best choice for caramelizing. But if you don't have a sweet onion there is a remedy. Sprinkle a few teaspoons of granulated sugar onto the onion in addition to salt and pepper. It will increase the sugar content enough to promote good browning.

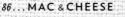

CREAMY LEEK MAC AND CHEESE

The delicate leek is my favorite member of the allium family. While leeks look like scallions on steroids, their flavor, especially when simmered in cream, is sweet and delicate. That's the way they are in this dish, which is an elegant side to any special dinner, especially roasted beef or lamb.

MAKES 4 TO 6 SERVINGS

$\frac{1}{2}$ cup (1 stick) unsalted butter, divided

3 large leeks, white parts only, halved, thinly sliced, and rinsed well

1 cup heavy cream, divided

Salt and freshly ground black pepper to taste

$\frac{1}{2}$ pound gemelli

3 tablespoons all-purpose flour

$1\frac{1}{2}$ cups whole milk, warmed

1 tablespoon Dijon mustard

Pinch of freshly grated nutmeg

4 ounces Gruyère, grated

4 ounces Emmental, grated

$\frac{3}{4}$ cup panko breadcrumbs

3 tablespoons freshly grated Parmesan

Heat 3 tablespoons of the butter in a skillet over medium heat. Add the leeks, and stir well to coat. Reduce the heat to medium-low, cover the pan, and cook the leeks for 10 minutes, stirring occasionally. Uncover the leeks, stir in $\frac{1}{2}$ cup of the cream, and season to taste with salt and pepper. Cook the leeks over low heat, stirring occasionally, for 10 minutes, or until they are very soft. Set aside.

Preheat the oven to 375°F. Grease a 13 x 9-inch baking pan.

Bring a pot of salted water to a boil over high heat. Cook the pasta until it is just beginning to soften to the al dente stage. Drain the pasta, run it under cold water, and return it to the pot.

Heat 3 tablespoons of the remaining butter in a saucepan over medium-low heat. Stir in the flour and cook, stirring constantly, for 1 minute, or until the mixture turns slightly beige, is bubbly, and appears to have grown in volume. Increase the heat to medium, and slowly whisk in the warm milk and remaining cream. Bring to a boil, whisking frequently. Whisk in the mustard and nutmeg, reduce the heat to low, and simmer the sauce for 2 minutes.

(continued)

Add the cheese to the sauce by $\frac{1}{2}$-cup measures, stirring until the cheese melts before making another addition. Pour the sauce over the pasta, add the leeks, and stir well. Season to taste with salt and pepper, and transfer the pasta to the prepared pan.

Melt the remaining 2 tablespoons of butter. Mix the butter with the breadcrumbs and Parmesan, and sprinkle the mixture over the top of the dish.

Bake the casserole for 20 to 30 minutes, or until the cheese sauce is bubbly and the crumbs on the top are deep brown. Allow to sit for 5 minutes, then serve.

Note: To prepare the dish in advance or reheat it, follow the instructions on page 26.

Variations:
- Substitute 6 ounces grated Cheddar and 2 ounces crumbled goat cheese for the Gruyère and Emmental.
- Substitute crushed canned fried onion rings for the panko breadcrumbs. Omit the butter if using onion rings.

LEEKS ARE THE LIKE THE CHARACTER PIGPEN IN THE COMIC strip *Peanuts*. They leave behind a cloud of dirt wherever they go. While you can get some of the grit off before slicing or dicing them, it's best to swirl sliced leeks around in a bowl of cold tap water. Pull them out with a sieve, and change the water a few times until it runs clean.

FAJITA MAC AND CHEESE

Adapted from Elbows Mac n' Cheese, Cerritos, CA

While at the restaurant the onion and pepper mixture tops the mac and cheese, I really prefer it folded in. The combination of cheeses and spices makes this a robust and bold dish perfect to serve with a Mexican meal.

MAKES 4 TO 6 SERVINGS

3 cups whole milk

1 small onion, halved

2 bay leaves

3 whole black peppercorns

1 clove

1/2 pound macaroni

1 tablespoon chili powder

1 tablespoon paprika

1 teaspoon ground cumin

1 teaspoon dried oregano, preferably Mexican

1/2 teaspoon crushed red pepper flakes

1/4 cup (1/2 stick) unsalted butter

1/3 cup all-purpose flour

4 ounces jalapeño Jack, grated, divided

(continued)

Bring the milk to a simmer over medium heat, stirring frequently to prevent it from boiling over. Add the onion, bay leaves, peppercorns, and clove to the milk. Allow the milk to steep for 30 minutes. Strain the milk, and discard the solids.

While the milk steeps, preheat the oven to 375°F. Grease a 13 x 9-inch baking pan.

Bring a pot of salted water to a boil over high heat. Cook the pasta until it is just beginning to soften to the al dente stage. Drain the pasta, run it under cold water, and return it to the pot.

Combine the chili powder, paprika, cumin, oregano, and red pepper flakes in a small bowl. Mix well, and set aside.

Heat the butter in a saucepan over medium-low heat. Stir in the flour and cook, stirring constantly, for 1 minute, or until the mixture turns slightly beige, is bubbly, and appears to have grown in volume. Increase the heat to medium, and slowly whisk in the steeped and strained milk. Bring to a boil, whisking frequently. Reduce the heat to low, and simmer the sauce for 2 minutes.

(continued)

8 ounces sharp Cheddar, grated

Pinch of freshly grated nutmeg

3 tablespoons olive oil, divided

1 medium onion, halved and thinly sliced

3 garlic cloves, minced, divided

1 roasted red bell pepper, seeded and thinly sliced

Salt and freshly ground black pepper to taste

$3/4$ cup panko breadcrumbs

2 tablespoons chopped fresh parsley

Lime wedges and tortilla chips, for serving

Reserve $1/2$ cup of the jalapeño Jack. Add the remaining cheeses to the sauce by $1/2$-cup measures, stirring until the cheese melts before making another addition. Stir in two-thirds of the seasoning mixture and all of the nutmeg.

Heat 1 tablespoon of the oil in a skillet over medium-high heat. Add the onion and 2 garlic cloves, and cook, stirring frequently, for 5 to 7 minutes, or until the onion is browned. Add the red pepper and remaining seasoning mix.

Pour the sauce over the pasta, add the onion mixture, and stir well. Season to taste with salt and pepper, and transfer the pasta to the prepared pan.

Combine the breadcrumbs, parsley, remaining garlic, and remaining olive oil in a small bowl. Season to taste with salt and pepper. Sprinkle the remaining cheese over the top of the dish, and then sprinkle with the breadcrumbs.

Bake the casserole for 20 to 30 minutes, or until the cheese sauce is bubbly and the crumbs on the top are deep brown. Allow to sit for 5 minutes, then serve, garnishing each serving with lime wedges and a few tortilla chips.

Note: To prepare the dish in advance or reheat it, follow the instructions on page 26.

MEXICAN OREGANO IS WIDELY AVAILABLE IN THE HISPANIC section of supermarkets and in Hispanic grocery stores. It has a more pungent aroma and flavor than its Mediterranean cousin, although both are part of the mint family. If using Mediterranean oregano, you might want to increase the amount by 20 percent to achieve the same vibrant flavor.

POBLANO CHILE MAC AND CHEESE

Poblano chiles, which are deep forest green, are the mildest of the chile family. They have only slightly more heat than a green bell pepper. But they add a wonderful aroma as well as flavor to this dish, which also contains some corn kernels and sliced olives for additional flavor and texture.

MAKES 4 TO 6 SERVINGS

2 poblano chiles

$^1/_2$ pound gemelli

$^1/_4$ cup ($^1/_2$ stick) unsalted butter

2 shallots, thinly sliced

2 garlic cloves, minced

3 tablespoons all-purpose flour

1 cup heavy cream, warmed

$^1/_2$ cup whole milk, warmed

3 ounces jalapeño Jack cheese, grated

3 ounces mild Cheddar, grated

$^3/_4$ cup cooked corn kernels

$^1/_4$ cup sliced pimiento-stuffed green olives

Salt and freshly ground black pepper to taste

1 cup crushed corn tortilla chips

2 tablespoons olive oil

2 tablespoons smoked Spanish paprika

2 teaspoons ground cumin

Preheat the oven broiler, and cover a broiler pan with heavy-duty aluminum foil. Prick the chiles at the stem end with the tip of a paring knife. Broil the chiles 6 inches from the broiler element for 3 to 4 minutes per side, turning them gently with tongs, or until the skin is black and charred. Place the chiles in a heavy resealable plastic bag to steam, and when cool enough to handle, rub off the skin and discard the seeds and stem. Cut the chiles into strips $^1/_2$-inch wide, and set aside.

Preheat the oven to 375°F. Grease a 13 x 9-inch baking pan.

Bring a pot of salted water to a boil over high heat. Cook the pasta until it is just beginning to soften to the al dente stage. Drain the pasta, run it under cold water, and return it to the pot.

Heat the butter in a saucepan over medium-low heat. Stir in the shallots and garlic, and cook, stirring frequently, for 3 minutes, or until the shallots are translucent. Stir in the flour and cook, stirring constantly, for 1 minute, or until the mixture turns slightly beige, is bubbly, and appears to have grown in volume. Increase the heat to medium, and slowly whisk in the warm cream and milk. Bring to a boil, whisking frequently. Reduce the heat to low, and simmer the sauce for 2 minutes.

(continued)

Add the cheese to the sauce by $1/2$-cup measures, stirring until the cheese melts before making another addition. Pour the sauce over the pasta, and stir well. Fold in the chiles, corn, and olives. Season to taste with salt and pepper, and transfer the pasta to the prepared pan.

Combine the crushed tortilla chips, olive oil, paprika, and cumin in a small bowl, and mix well. Sprinkle the mixture over the top of the dish. Bake the casserole for 20 to 30 minutes, or until the cheese sauce is bubbly and the crumbs on the top are deep brown. Allow to sit for 5 minutes, then serve.

Note: To prepare the dish in advance or reheat it, follow the instructions on page 26.

PAPRIKA IS A POWDER MADE BY GRINDING AROMATIC SWEET red pepper pods several times. The color can vary from deep red to bright orange, and the flavor ranges from mild to pungent and hot. Unlike many spices, it's used in a wide variety of cuisines, ranging from Hungarian to Spanish. One subset of paprika is smoked Spanish paprika, called *pimenton de la vera*. The peppers are first smoked over oak wood, and the aroma of the smoke does not dissipate when the dish is cooked.

Chapter 4:

FRUITS DE MER

As mac and cheese leaves the school cafeteria and takes its place on upscale restaurant menus, it begins to rub shoulders with luxury ingredients. The two you'll find most often when cooking the recipes in this book are those prized crustaceans: lobster and shrimp.

Lobster mac and cheese is now a national trend, and you'll find many recipes for it in this chapter. Lobster has a delicate and inherently sweet flavor, so the cheeses used with it need to be on the milder side to not overpower the lobster. While the recipes are written for lobster, cooked shrimp or lump crabmeat can be substituted in any of these recipes. So can small cubes of cooked white-fleshed fish fillets such as halibut or cod.

In addition to seafood, you'll find a few recipes in this chapter for other species of fish. And the chapter concludes with an updated version of Tuna Noodle Casserole. While it's crowned with a topping of crispy potato chips, that's where the similarity to the oft-mocked classic (made with canned cream of mushroom soup) ends.

Cooking Lobster and Lobster Stock

I'M VERY LUCKY BECAUSE MOST FISH MARKETS IN NEW ENGLAND sell precooked lobster meat. It's a win-win situation; they have lobsters in the tank that they know are ready to go on Social Security, and they can salvage the lobster meat and fetch a premium price for it.

However, except in an emergency, I always prefer to cook lobsters myself. That way the meat can be slightly undercooked so that it doesn't toughen in the mac and cheese, plus I'll have the bodies available to make stock. If you are squeamish about cooking lobster and still remember the scene from the film *Annie Hall*, I'll give you some pointers to make the task easier.

Cooking Lobsters

When you purchase lobsters, you want them to be frisky as they come out of the tank. Lobsters can stay alive in a tank for many days after they're pulled from the ocean, but they slow down considerably. If they're barely moving, ask to see another one, or go to another store.

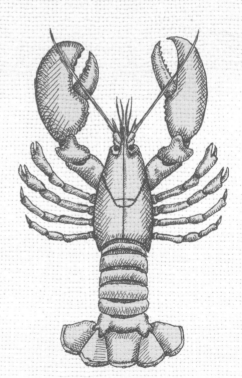

Lobsters are frequently packed in seaweed, so ask the fish store if any is available. It gives the true taste of the sea to the lobsters if they're cooked with it.

Almost all the lobsters you buy are small ones, called "chicken lobsters." They range in size from $1\frac{1}{4}$ to $1\frac{1}{2}$ pounds. To cook them, bring a large pot of salted water to a boil over high heat. Hold the lobster on its back, and insert it into the boiling water head first. Cover the pot, and bring the water back to a boil as quickly as possible.

The shell of the lobster turns bright red long before the meat is cooked through, so time is the only test of doneness. If you are cooking a lobster to eat on its own, cook 13 to 15 minutes after the water returns to a boil. However, for these recipes I'm recommending that they be removed after 12 minutes. The meat will still be slightly translucent, but it will cook further in the dish.

Cool the lobster under cold running water. Discard the rubber bands, and break the legs and claws off the body. For large lobsters, it's worth the extra work of getting out choice tidbits of meat from the small walking legs and body, but for small lobsters, the goal is to extract the meat from the tail, claws, and arms, and then use the rest for making stock.

If you don't have a lobster cracker, place a folded paper towel over the claws and hit them with a hammer. To gain access to the prized tail meat, just twist it off the body and pull the meat out with a seafood fork.

Seafood Stock

Once you've picked the meat from the lobster, it's time to make stock from its remains. While only one of the recipes in this chapter uses stock as an ingredient, it's a crime to just toss out the body. Lobster stock is such a wonderful ingredient to use in soups and sauces.

Discard the feathery gills from the outside of the body cavity and the small sack found at the top of the head. Break all shell fragments into small pieces with a lobster cracker, strong knife, or hammer. Cut the small walking legs into 1-inch segments, and break apart the body into small pieces.

LOBSTER STOCK

MAKES 2 CUPS

Shells and other remains
  from 1 lobster (see above)

1 small onion, sliced

1 small carrot, sliced

1 celery rib, sliced

2 sprigs fresh parsley

1 sprig fresh thyme
  (substitute 1 teaspoon
  dried)

1 bay leaf

12 black peppercorns

Cover the lobster shell fragments with 2 quarts of water. Bring to a boil over high heat. Reduce the heat to low and simmer the stock, uncovered, for $1^{1}/_{4}$ hours.

Strain the stock, and return it to the pot. Add the onion, carrot, celery, parsley, thyme, bay leaf, and peppercorns. Bring the stock to a boil over high heat, then reduce the heat to low and simmer the stock, uncovered, for 45 minutes. Strain the stock, pressing with the back of a spoon to extract as much liquid as possible. Return the stock to the pot, and reduce over medium heat until 2 cups remain.

Note: The stock can be refrigerated for up to 5 days or frozen for up to 3 months.

Variation: Substitute shells from 3 pounds of raw shrimp for the lobster shells.

MASCARPONE LOBSTER MAC AND CHEESE

Adapted from DiMillo's on the Water, Portland, ME

Tony DiMillo started his first restaurant on a wharf in Portland in 1954, and his slogan was, "The clams you eat here today slept last night in Casco Bay." The DiMillo family is still running this popular spot, although chef Melissa Bouchard now oversees the cooking. The menu continues to stress the region's pristine seafood, but also includes some Italian specialties. The mac and cheese is topped with the same mixture used on DiMillo's famous stuffed lobster.

MAKES 4 TO 6 SERVINGS

$1/2$ pound farfalle

6 tablespoons unsalted butter, divided

1 garlic clove, minced

2 tablespoons Cognac

1 cup lobster stock or shellfish stock (page 97)

12 ounces mascarpone

3 tablespoons freshly grated Parmesan

5 ounces cooked lobster meat, diced

Salt and freshly ground black pepper to taste

1 small shallot, minced

1 tablespoon finely chopped red or yellow bell pepper

(continued)

Preheat the oven to 375°F. Grease a 13 x 9-inch baking pan.

Bring a pot of salted water to a boil over high heat. Cook the pasta until it is just beginning to soften to the al dente stage. Drain the pasta, run it under cold water, and return it to the pot.

Heat 2 tablespoons of the butter in a saucepan over medium heat. Add the garlic, and cook for 30 seconds. Add the Cognac and cook for 1 minute, or until the liquid is almost evaporated. Add the stock, and bring to a boil. Cook until the liquid is reduced by half. Whisk in the mascarpone and Parmesan.

Pour the sauce over the pasta, and stir well. Fold in the lobster, season to taste with salt and pepper, and transfer the pasta to the prepared pan.

Melt the remaining butter in a skillet over medium heat. Add the shallot and bell pepper, and cook over low heat, stirring frequently, for 5 minutes. Add the sherry and mustard, and cook for 2 minutes. Stir in the bread-

(continued)

1 tablespoon dry sherry

¼ teaspoon dry mustard powder

1½ cups panko bread-crumbs

crumbs, and mix well. Season the crumb mixture to taste with salt and pepper. Sprinkle the crumbs over the top of the dish.

Bake the casserole for 20 to 30 minutes, or until the cheese sauce is bubbly and the crumbs on the top are deep brown. Allow to sit for 5 minutes, then serve.

Note: To prepare the dish in advance or reheat it, follow the instructions on page 26.

ALTHOUGH THERE IS NO DIFFERENCE IN THE FLAVOR OF A MALE or female lobster, the bright red roe from the females adds a rosy color to stocks and can be sprinkled over salads as a garnish. To learn how to identify the female, ask your fishmonger to show you two lobsters of similar size—one male and one female. The one with the broader abdomen and tail is the female. The female also has smaller, more flexible swimmerets, which are the first pair of legs at the base of the tail.

LOBSTER MAC AND CHEESE WITH TARRAGON

Adapted from Seastar Restaurant & Raw Bar, Seattle, WA

Chef John Howie, who began the Seastar in Seattle in 2002 and now has an offshoot in nearby Bellevue, has been part of the dining scene in the Northwest for more than two decades. He was formerly chef at the Palisade Restaurant in Seattle, which featured Hawaiian influences. The chef is also the author of *Passion & Palate: Recipes for a Generous Table.*

MAKES 4 TO 6 SERVINGS

$^{1}/_{2}$ pound macaroni

$^{1}/_{4}$ cup ($^{1}/_{2}$ stick) unsalted butter

$^{1}/_{4}$ cup finely chopped onion

$2^{1}/_{2}$ cups heavy cream

3 ounces fontina, grated

1 tablespoon chopped fresh tarragon

6 ounces cooked lobster meat, diced

Salt and freshly ground black pepper to taste

$^{1}/_{2}$ cup toasted plain breadcrumbs

1 ounce Cheddar, grated

1 ounce Asiago, grated

Bring a pot of salted water to a boil over high heat. Cook the pasta until it is al dente. Drain the pasta, run it under cold water, and return it to the pot.

Heat the butter in a saucepan over medium-low heat. Add the onion and cook, stirring frequently, for 5 minutes, or until the onion softens. Do not let it brown. Increase the heat to medium-high, and stir in the cream. Bring to a boil, whisking frequently. Reduce the heat to low, and simmer the sauce for 15 minutes, or until reduced by one-third.

Add the fontina to the sauce by $^{1}/_{2}$-cup measures, stirring until the cheese melts before making another addition. Stir in the tarragon.

Preheat the oven broiler. Grease a 13 x 9-inch baking pan.

Add the sauce to the pasta, and stir well. Fold in the lobster, and season to taste with salt and pepper. Transfer the pasta to the prepared pan. Combine the breadcrumbs, Cheddar, and Asiago, and sprinkle it over the top of the dish. Broil the dish 6 to 8 inches from the

2 ounces (4 to 6 thin slices)
    Délice de Bourgogne
    (substitute Explorateur or
    Saint André), for serving

2 tablespoons chopped
    fresh chervil, for serving

broiler element for 1 to 2 minutes, or until the cheeses brown. Serve immediately, garnishing each serving with a slice of Délice de Bourgogne and some chervil.

Note: The sauce can be prepared up to 2 days in advance and refrigerated. Bring it to a simmer over low heat. Do not cook the pasta until just prior to serving.

LOBSTER MAC AND CHEESE WITH MARINATED TOMATOES

Adapted from The Fat Cat Restaurant, Quincy, MA

After extensive research, Quincy native Neil Kiley decided to open a restaurant in his hometown, a suburb of Boston, in 2008. The loyal following of this spot, with exposed brick walls and a large painting of an orange-eyed cat, are devoted to the repetoire of chef Thomas Coleman who heads the kitchen staff. His version of lobster mac and cheese is made with a combination of four cheeses and topped with flavorful marinated tomatoes, as well as crunchy panko.

MAKES 4 TO 6 SERVINGS

$^1/_2$ pound cavatappi

2 ripe plum tomatoes, cored, seeded, and sliced

1 tablespoon chopped fresh basil (substitute $^1/_2$ teaspoon dried)

2 garlic cloves, minced, divided

2 tablespoons dry white wine

Salt and freshly ground black pepper to taste

2 tablespoons olive oil

2 cups heavy cream

4 ounces freshly grated Parmesan, divided

2 ounces Manchego, grated

2 ounces blue cheese, crumbled

2 ounces white Cheddar, grated

Preheat the oven to 375°F. Grease a 13 x 9-inch baking pan.

Bring a pot of salted water to a boil over high heat. Cook the pasta until it is just beginning to soften to the al dente stage. Drain the pasta, run it under cold water, and return it to the pot.

While the pasta cooks, lay the tomatoes out on a plate. Sprinkle them with the basil, half of the garlic, and the wine. Season to taste with salt and pepper, and set aside.

Heat the oil in a skillet over medium-high heat. Add the remaining garlic, and cook for 30 seconds. Add the cream, and bring to a boil, stirring frequently. Reduce the heat to low, and simmer the cream for 2 minutes.

Reserve half of the Parmesan. Add the remaining Parmesan and other cheeses to the cream by $^1/_2$-cup measures, stirring until the cheese melts before making another addition.

Pour the sauce over the pasta, and stir well. Fold in the lobster, season to taste with salt and pepper, and transfer the pasta to the prepared pan. Top the pasta with the tomato slices. Mix the reserved Parmesan and breadcrumbs together, and sprinkle it over the top of the dish.

5 ounces cooked lobster
  meat, diced

$\frac{1}{2}$ cup panko breadcrumbs

Bake the casserole for 20 to 30 minutes, or until the cheese sauce is bubbly and the crumbs on the top are deep brown. Allow to sit for 5 minutes, then serve.

Note: To prepare the dish in advance or reheat it, follow the instructions on page 26.

NEXT TO FRANCE AND ITALY, SPAIN PRODUCES THE MOST CHEESES in Europe, and Manchego is the most famous. It comes from La Mancha, the land of Cervantes' Don Quixote, and is made from sheep's milk. It is ivory in color and has an almost nutty aroma and flavor.

TRUFFLED LOBSTER MAC AND CHEESE WITH MUSHROOMS AND TOMATO

Adapted from Lady Gregory's, Chicago, IL

Lady Gregory's, which opened in 2011 in the Andersonville section of Chicago, is an upscale Irish pub that boasts a whiskey list of more than three hundred options. It's named for Isabella Augusta Persse, later Lady Gregory, who co-founded the Irish Literary Theater with William Butler Yeats in 1899. Owned by Munster Taverns, the same company that owns Wilde Bar & Restaurant, Lady Gregory's serves this elaborate version of now-popular lobster mac and cheese as a signature dish.

MAKES 4 TO 6 SERVINGS

- 1/2 pound cavatappi
- 1/4 cup (1/2 stick) unsalted butter, divided
- 2 ounces fresh shiitake mushrooms, stemmed and sliced
- 2 ounces fresh Portobello mushrooms, stemmed and diced
- 3 garlic cloves, minced, divided
- 1 teaspoon fresh thyme (substitute 1/8 teaspoon dried)
- Salt and freshly ground black pepper to taste
- 3 tablespoons dry white wine
- 3 ripe plum tomatoes, cored, seeded, and diced

Preheat the oven to 375°F. Grease a 13 x 9-inch baking pan.

Bring a pot of salted water to a boil over high heat. Cook the pasta until it is just beginning to soften to the al dente stage. Drain the pasta, run it under cold water, and return it to the pot.

Heat 3 tablespoons of the butter in a large skillet over medium-high heat. Add the shiitake mushrooms, Portobello mushrooms, two-thirds of the garlic, and thyme. Season to taste with salt and pepper. Cook, stirring frequently, for 5 to 7 minutes, or until the liquid evaporates and the mushrooms brown. Add the wine and tomatoes, and cook for 2 minutes, or until the wine almost evaporates. Whisk in the cream. Bring to a boil, whisking frequently. Reduce the heat to low, and simmer the sauce for 2 minutes.

Add the cheese to the sauce by 1/2-cup measures, stirring until the cheese melts before making another addition. Pour the sauce over the pasta, and stir well. Fold in the lobster and 1 tablespoon of the truffle oil. Season to

2 cups heavy cream

8 ounces sharp Cheddar, grated

6 ounces cooked lobster meat, diced

2 tablespoons white truffle oil, divided

1/4 cup chopped white onion

3/4 cup crumbled cornbread

taste with salt and pepper, and transfer the pasta to the prepared pan.

Melt the remaining butter in a small skillet, and add the onion and remaining garlic. Cook, stirring frequently, for 3 minutes, or until the onion is translucent. Mix in the crumbled cornbread, and sprinkle it over the top of the dish.

Bake the casserole for 20 to 30 minutes, or until the cheese sauce is bubbly and the crumbs on the top are deep brown. Drizzle the remaining truffle oil over the top. Allow to sit for 5 minutes, then serve.

Note: To prepare the dish in advance or reheat it, follow the instructions on page 26.

WITH ALMOST ALL FRESH HERBS, THE SUBSTITUTION RATIO FOR the dried form is 1 tablespoon fresh to 1 teaspoon dried. One exception to this, however, is thyme. The leaves are so small once dried that I've found that 1/2 teaspoon dried produces the same flavor as 1 tablespoon fresh.

SPICY SHRIMP MAC AND CHEESE

Adapted from Co Co. Sala, Washington, D.C.

The name stands for the two prime ingredients featured on the menu—chocolate and coffee—*sala* being the Italian word for "lounge." Co Co. Sala, which opened in 2008, is a chocoholic's fantasy come true. The kitchen is headed up by Santosh Tiptur, a native of India who was formerly executive pastry chef at the Ritz-Carlton Hotel in San Juan, Puerto Rico. While the décor features spun sugar sculptures and the menu includes flights of dishes like chocolate-covered bacon, there is a small segment of savory dishes for those in need of sustenance prior to the sugar rush, and one of the most popular is this spicy mac and cheese.

MAKES 4 TO 6 SERVINGS

$1/2$ pound small penne

2 tablespoons unsalted butter

1 small onion, chopped and divided

1 bay leaf

2 tablespoons all-purpose flour

2 cups whole milk, warmed

2 ounces Gruyère, grated, divided

$1^{1}/2$ ounces jalapeño Jack, grated

$1^{1}/2$ ounces freshly grated Parmesan

Pinch of freshly grated nutmeg

2 tablespoons olive oil

3 garlic cloves, minced

Preheat the oven to 375°F. Grease a 13 x 9-inch baking pan.

Bring a pot of salted water to a boil over high heat. Cook the pasta until it is just beginning to soften to the al dente stage. Drain the pasta, run it under cold water, and return it to the pot.

Heat the butter in a saucepan over medium-low heat. Stir in 2 tablespoons of the onion and the bay leaf, and cook, stirring occasionally, for 2 minutes. Stir in the flour and cook, stirring constantly, for 1 minute, or until the mixture turns slightly beige, is bubbly, and appears to have grown in volume. Increase the heat to medium, and slowly whisk in the warm milk. Bring to a boil, whisking frequently. Reduce the heat to low, and simmer the sauce for 2 minutes.

Reserve $1/2$ cup of the Gruyère. Add the remaining cheeses to the sauce by $1/2$-cup measures, stirring until the cheese melts before making another addition. Stir in the nutmeg. Remove and discard the bay leaf. Set aside.

Heat the olive oil in a skillet over medium-high heat. Add the remaining onion and garlic, and cook, stirring

2 jalapeño or serrano
chiles, seeds and ribs
removed, finely chopped

1$\frac{1}{2}$ teaspoons Cajun
seasoning

$\frac{1}{2}$ teaspoon ground cumin

$\frac{1}{2}$ teaspoon ground
coriander

1 ripe plum tomato, cored
and diced

4 ounces medium raw
shrimp, peeled and
deveined

1$\frac{1}{2}$ teaspoons freshly
squeezed lemon juice

2 tablespoons chopped
fresh cilantro

Salt and freshly ground
black pepper to taste

$\frac{1}{2}$ cup plain breadcrumbs

frequently, for 3 minutes, or until the onion is translucent.
Add the chiles, Cajun seasoning, cumin, and coriander,
and cook for 1 minute, stirring constantly. Add the
tomato and cook for 2 minutes, or until the vegetables
soften. Add the shrimp, lemon juice, and cilantro, and
cook for 2 minutes, or until the shrimp are pink.

Pour the sauce over the pasta, and stir well. Fold in the
shrimp mixture, season to taste with salt and pepper, and
transfer the pasta to the prepared pan. Mix the reserved
Gruyère and breadcrumbs together, and sprinkle it over
the top of the dish.

Bake the casserole for 20 to 30 minutes, or until the
cheese sauce is bubbly and the crumbs on the top are
deep brown. Allow to sit for 5 minutes, then serve.

Note: To prepare the dish in advance or reheat it, follow
the instructions on page 26.

IT'S COMMON TO SEE JALAPENO AND SERRANO CHILES GIVEN
as recipe options in the same quantity, although serrano peppers are much smaller.
They are also much hotter, so the larger jalapeño and the small serrano produce the
same amount of heat.

SHRIMP SCAMPI MAC AND CHEESE

Adapted from Cheese-ology Macaroni & Cheese, St. Louis, MO

Cheese-ology is a trailblazer in its region for having an all-mac menu. Chef and owner Bill Courtney decided to leave his job as a medical researcher after more than a decade, and fell in love with the all-mac concept when visiting places such as Macbar and S'MAC in New York. His storefront spot is right near Washington University, and all its hungry students. He keeps the cheeses in this dish mild so that the lemon and garlicky flavor of the shrimp emerge.

MAKES 4 TO 6 SERVINGS

$1/2$ pound macaroni

6 tablespoons unsalted butter, divided

8 ounces medium raw shrimp, peeled and deveined

3 garlic cloves, minced

Salt to taste

1 teaspoon lemon pepper seasoning

$1/4$ cup all-purpose flour

2 cups whole milk, warmed

$1/4$ teaspoon freshly grated nutmeg

4 ounces whole-milk mozzarella, grated

3 ounces mild provolone, grated

1 ounce freshly grated Parmesan cheese

Freshly ground black pepper to taste

$1/2$ cup panko breadcrumbs

Preheat the oven to 375°F. Grease a 13 x 9-inch baking pan.

Bring a pot of salted water to a boil over high heat. Cook the pasta until it is just beginning to soften to the al dente stage. Drain the pasta, run it under cold water, and return it to the pot.

Heat 2 tablespoons of the butter in a skillet over medium-high heat. Add the shrimp and garlic and cook, stirring frequently, for 4 to 5 minutes, or until the shrimp are pink. Season to taste with salt and lemon pepper. Add the shrimp to the pan with the pasta.

Heat the remaining butter in a saucepan over medium-low heat. Stir in the flour and cook, stirring constantly, for 1 minute, or until the mixture turns slightly beige, is bubbly, and appears to have grown in volume. Increase the heat to medium, and slowly whisk in the warm milk. Bring to a boil, whisking frequently. Reduce the heat to low, stir in the nutmeg, and simmer the sauce for 2 minutes.

Add the cheese to the sauce by $1/2$-cup measures, stirring until the cheese melts before making another addition. Pour the sauce over the pasta, and stir well. Season to taste with salt and pepper, and transfer the pasta to the prepared pan. Sprinkle the breadcrumbs over the top of the dish.

Bake the casserole for 20 to 30 minutes, or until the cheese sauce is bubbly and the crumbs on the top are deep brown. Allow to sit for 5 minutes, then serve.

Note: To prepare the dish in advance or reheat it, follow the instructions on page 26.

DO NOT EQUATE THE WORDS "FRESH SHRIMP" WITH SHRIMP that have never been frozen. Truth be told, you probably will be unable to find never-frozen shrimp fresh from the ocean these days unless you have a shrimper friend or net it yourself. This is not necessarily a bad thing. Nowadays, shrimp is harvested, cleaned, and flash-frozen on the boats before they ever reach the shore. But if you buy shrimp that you plan to freeze, ask the fishmonger to sell you some still frozen rather than thawed in the case. When you keep thawing and refreezing shrimp it breaks down the cell fibers and they can become mushy.

MAC AND CHEESE ALLA AJILLO

Adapted from MacDaddy's Mac & Cheese Bar, Monroe, CT

Monroe is a sleepy village in popular Fairfield County, and serves as a bed-room community for people who work in New York and nearby Stamford, Connecticut. MacDaddy's opened in 2011, and offers snack-sized portions of its twenty-plus dishes. One of the most popular is this shrimp version, which includes a bit of sherry, as well as a combination of cheeses.

MAKES 4 TO 6 SERVINGS

1/2 pound macaroni

1 tablespoon olive oil

1 garlic clove, minced

4 ounces raw small shrimp, peeled and deveined

1 tablespoon cream sherry

1 teaspoon freshly squeezed lemon juice

Salt and freshly ground black pepper to taste

1/4 cup (1/2 stick) unsalted butter

2 tablespoons all-purpose flour

2 cups whole milk, warmed

3 ounces Asiago, grated

2 ounces whole-milk mozzarella, grated

Bring a pot of salted water to a boil over high heat. Cook the pasta until it is al dente. Drain the pasta, run it under cold water, and return it to the pot.

Heat the oil in a skillet over medium-high heat. Add the garlic and cook for 30 seconds. Add the shrimp and cook for 2 to 3 minutes, or until the shrimp are pink. Add the sherry and lemon juice, and cook for 1 minute. Season to taste with salt and pepper, and set aside.

Heat the butter in a saucepan over medium-low heat. Stir in the flour and cook, stirring constantly, for 1 minute, or until the mixture turns slightly beige, is bubbly, and appears to have grown in volume. Increase the heat to medium, and slowly whisk in the warm milk. Bring to a boil, whisking frequently. Reduce the heat to low, and simmer the sauce for 2 minutes.

Add the cheese to the sauce by 1/2-cup measures, stirring until the cheese melts before making another addition. Add the sauce to the pasta, and stir well. Fold in the shrimp mixture, and season to taste with salt and pepper. Cook over low heat until the pasta is hot and coated with the sauce. Serve immediately.

Note: The sauce, with the shrimp mixture folded in, can be prepared up to 2 days in advance and refrigerated. Bring it to a simmer over low heat. Do not cook the pasta until just prior to serving.

THE WAY YOU TREAT GARLIC DETERMINES THE INTENSITY OF its flavor. Pushing the cloves through a garlic press is the way to extract the most punch. Mincing the cloves once they're peeled produces a milder flavor.

CHESAPEAKE CRAB MAC AND CHEESE

Adapted from The Nook, Charlottesville, VA

Charlottesville is known for the Jeffersonian architecture of the University of Virginia, and it's also a tourist destination on the East Coast. The building in which The Nook is housed dates from the 1880s, and there has been a restaurant on the ground floor since 1912. During the winter months there is a special mac and cheese menu, and this succulent dish with lump crabmeat is one of the most popular dishes.

MAKES 4 TO 6 SERVINGS

$^1/_2$ pound fusilli

$^1/_4$ cup ($^1/_2$ stick) unsalted butter

$^1/_4$ cup all-purpose flour

2 cups whole milk, warmed

3 ounces mild yellow Cheddar, grated

2 ounces Monterey Jack, grated

1$^1/_2$ ounces Asiago, grated

1$^1/_2$ teaspoons Old Bay seasoning

Pinch of freshly grated nutmeg

3 ripe plum tomatoes, cored, seeded, and diced

6 ounces lump crabmeat, picked over well

Salt and freshly ground black pepper to taste

Bring a pot of salted water to a boil over high heat. Cook the pasta until it is al dente. Drain the pasta, run it under cold water, and return it to the pot.

Heat the butter in a saucepan over medium-low heat. Stir in the flour and cook, stirring constantly, for 1 minute, or until the mixture turns slightly beige, is bubbly, and appears to have grown in volume. Increase the heat to medium, and slowly whisk in the warm milk. Bring to a boil, whisking frequently. Reduce the heat to low, and simmer the sauce for 2 minutes.

Add the cheese to the sauce by $^1/_2$-cup measures, stirring until the cheese melts before making another addition. Add the Old Bay, nutmeg, and tomatoes to the sauce, and simmer for 1 minute.

Add the sauce to the pasta, and stir well. Gently fold in the crabmeat, and season to taste with salt and pepper. Cook over low heat until the pasta is hot and coated with the sauce. Serve immediately.

Note: The sauce can be prepared up to 2 days in advance and refrigerated. Bring it to a simmer over low heat. Do not cook the pasta until just prior to serving.

NEW ENGLAND CLAM MAC AND CHEESE

This recipe has all the wonderful creaminess of a classic New England chowder, but the subtle cheese makes it even richer and more delicious. A key to the mild seafood flavor is reduced clam juice.

MAKES 4 TO 6 SERVINGS

1/2 pound macaroni

1 pint fresh minced clams

1 (8-ounce) bottle clam juice

2 tablespoons chopped fresh parsley

1 teaspoon fresh thyme (substitute 1/4 teaspoon dried)

6 tablespoons unsalted butter, divided

1 medium onion, diced

2 celery ribs, diced

1/4 cup all-purpose flour

2 cups heavy cream, warmed

4 ounces fontina, grated

2 ounces mascarpone

Salt and freshly ground black pepper to taste

3/4 cup crushed saltines

Preheat the oven to 375°F. Grease a 13 x 9-inch baking pan.

Bring a pot of salted water to a boil over high heat. Cook the pasta until it is just beginning to soften to the al dente stage. Drain the pasta, run it under cold water, and return it to the pot.

Drain the clams and reserve the juice, pressing them with the back of a spoon to extract as much of the clam juice as possible. Refrigerate the clams, and transfer the clam juice to a saucepan. Add the bottled clam juice, and bring to a boil over high heat. Reduce the heat to medium, and add the parsley and thyme. Cook, stirring occasionally, until the liquid is reduced by two-thirds.

Heat 4 tablespoons of the butter in a saucepan over medium-low heat. Add the onion and celery, and cook, stirring frequently, for 5 to 7 minutes, or until the vegetables soften. Stir in the flour and cook, stirring constantly, for 1 minute, or until the mixture turns slightly beige, is bubbly, and appears to have grown in volume. Increase the heat to medium, and slowly whisk in the reduced clam juice and the warm cream. Bring to a boil, whisking frequently. Reduce the heat to low, and simmer the sauce for 2 minutes.

Add the clams, and cook for 2 minutes, or until the clams are cooked. Add the cheese to the sauce by $^1\!/_2$-cup measures, stirring until the cheese melts before making another addition.

Pour the sauce over the pasta, and stir well. Season to taste with salt and pepper, and transfer the pasta to the prepared pan. Melt the remaining butter, and mix it with the cracker crumbs. Sprinkle the mixture over the top of the dish.

Bake the casserole for 20 to 30 minutes, or until the cheese sauce is bubbly and the crumbs on the top are deep brown. Allow to sit for 5 minutes, then serve.

Note: To prepare the dish in advance or reheat it, follow the instructions on page 26.

Variations:
- Add $^1\!/_2$ cup crumbled bacon to the dish, and substitute 2 tablespoons bacon grease for 2 tablespoons of the butter.
- Substitute 6 ounces cooked cod, halibut, or any white-fleshed fish fillet for the clams. Fold the fish gently into the dish after the sauce has been added to the macaroni and stirred well. Also, substitute $1^1\!/_2$ cups of fish stock for the clam juice.

FRESH MINCED CLAMS ARE FOUND TODAY IN ALMOST EVERY supermarket, either in the fish case or frozen. But if you turn to canned clams for this or any other recipe, add them to the dish without any further cooking because they're already cooked and will become rubbery.

DILLED SALMON MAC AND CHEESE

This is a wonderful dish for parties because it's both elegant and easy to eat. I've always been fond of adding aromatic fresh dill to creamed salmon dishes, and including little bits of smoked salmon creates a far more complex flavor.

MAKES 4 TO 6 SERVINGS

1/2 pound campanelle

1/4 cup (1/2 stick) unsalted butter, divided

4 ounces fresh salmon fillet, skinned

Salt and freshly ground black pepper to taste

2 shallots, minced

3 tablespoons all-purpose flour

2 cups half-and-half, warmed

3 tablespoons chopped fresh dill

2 tablespoons freshly squeezed lemon juice

1 teaspoon grated lemon zest

6 ounces mascarpone

2 ounces freshly grated Parmesan

1 ounce smoked salmon, chopped

Preheat the oven to 400°F. Bring a pot of salted water to a boil. Cook the pasta until it is al dente. Drain the pasta, run it under cold water, and return it to the pot.

Melt 1 tablespoon of the butter, and rub it on both sides of the salmon. Season the salmon with salt and pepper, and enclose it in a square of aluminum foil. Bake for 10 to 12 minutes, or until it is cooked through and flakes easily. When cool enough to handle, break the salmon into 1-inch pieces.

Heat the remaining butter in a saucepan over medium-low heat. Add the shallots, and cook, stirring frequently, for 5 minutes, or until they soften. Stir in the flour and cook, stirring constantly, for 1 minute, or until the mixture turns slightly beige, is bubbly, and appears to have grown in volume. Increase the heat to medium, and slowly whisk in the half-and-half. Bring to a boil, whisking frequently. Reduce the heat to low, and simmer for 2 minutes.

Stir in the dill, lemon juice, and lemon zest. Add the cheese to the sauce by 1/2-cup measures, stirring until the cheese melts before making another addition. Stir in the smoked salmon, and simmer for 1 minute.

Add the sauce to the pasta, and stir well. Gently fold in the salmon, and season to taste with salt and pepper. Cook over low heat until the pasta is hot and coated with the sauce. Serve immediately.

Note: The sauce can be prepared up to 2 days in advance and refrigerated. Bring it to a simmer over low heat. Do not cook the pasta until just prior to serving.

TUNA NOODLE CASSEROLE

There's nothing wrong with this cafeteria standard that replacing the can of cream of mushroom with a porcini cheese sauce doesn't fix. It's still topped with crushed potato chips, and while your childhood memories might not include sautéed vegetables, they certainly enhance both the flavor and texture.

MAKES 4 TO 6 SERVINGS

- ½ pound curly egg noodles
- ½ cup dried porcini mushrooms
- ½ cup seafood stock or chicken stock, heated to boiling
- ¼ cup (½ stick) unsalted butter, divided
- 1 small onion, diced
- 2 celery ribs, diced
- 3 tablespoons all-purpose flour
- 2 cups whole milk, warmed
- 2 tablespoons dry sherry
- ½ teaspoon fresh thyme (substitute a pinch dried)
- 2 ounces whole-milk mozzarella cheese, grated
- 2 (5-ounce) cans chunk tuna packed in water, drained and broken into chunks

Preheat the oven to 375°F. Grease a 13 x 9-inch baking pan.

Bring a pot of salted water to a boil over high heat. Cook the noodles until they are just beginning to soften to the al dente stage. Drain the noodles, run them under cold water, and return them to the pot.

Soak the mushrooms in the boiling-hot stock for 10 minutes, pushing them down into the liquid with the back of a spoon. Drain the mushrooms, reserving the stock. Chop the mushrooms, and set aside. Strain the stock through a sieve lined with a paper coffee filter or paper towel, and set aside.

Melt 2 tablespoons of the butter in a saucepan over medium heat. Add the onion and celery, and cook, stirring frequently, for 5 to 7 minutes, or until the vegetables soften. Scrape the vegetables into the pot with the noodles.

Return the saucepan to the stove, and melt the remaining butter over medium-low heat. Stir in the flour and cook, stirring constantly, for 1 minute, or until the mixture turns slightly beige, is bubbly, and appears to have grown in volume.

Increase the heat to medium, and slowly whisk in the warm milk, reserved stock, sherry, and thyme. Bring to a boil, whisking frequently. Stir in the mushrooms, reduce the heat to low, and simmer the sauce for 2 minutes, or

¾ cup frozen peas, thawed (optional)

Salt and freshly ground black pepper to taste

1 (1.5-ounce) bag potato chips, crushed

until thickened. Add the cheese to the sauce by ½-cup measures, stirring until the cheese melts before making another addition.

Pour the sauce over the noodles, and stir well. Gently fold in the tuna and peas, if using. Season to taste with salt and pepper, and transfer the mixture to the prepared pan. Sprinkle crushed potato chips over the top of the dish.

Bake the casserole for 20 to 30 minutes, or until the sauce is bubbly and the crumbs on the top are deep brown. Allow to sit for 5 minutes, then serve.

Note: To prepare the dish in advance or reheat it, follow the instructions on page 26.

IN THE PAST FEW YEARS, CANS OF TUNA HAVE BEEN SUBJECTED to the same downsizing as other shelf-stable foods. They're now five ounces and not the previous six, in the same way that a one-pound can of beans is now fifteen ounces and cans of tomatoes shrank even more. While this dish was formulated using the smaller can size, if your old recipes call for a few cans of tuna, you may consider adding an additional can.

Chapter 6

MEATY MACS

Casseroles featuring pasta and cheese with meats have held a revered place on the tables of potluck suppers for generations, including ubiquitous lasagna and cheddar mac and cheese with some ham thrown in for good measure. But any dish that requires layering takes time. To the rescue come the recipes in this chapter. All of them are fairly hearty, but they are also quick and easy to make.

These dishes are a wonderful way to transform last night's roast chicken into a new and exciting dish rather than a leftover, especially if there really isn't enough meat remaining to feed the family.

The number of portions given is for side dish servings, as is true with all the recipes in this book. However, there are two ways to transform them into an entrée. The most obvious one is to double the recipe. But another option is to increase the amount of meat or poultry. If you double the amount of meat, it will not affect the cooking time or the consistency of the dish, but it will make the dish heartier and more filling.

CHICKEN AND BROCCOLI MAC AND CHEESE

This is a lighter dish than most mac and cheese recipes because the sauce is made with reduced stock in addition to dairy products. In classic French sauce-making it's referred to as a velouté rather than a Mornay.

MAKES 4 TO 6 SERVINGS

2 cups chicken stock, preferably homemade

1/2 pound fresh broccoli crowns, cut into 3/4-inch florets

1/2 pound cavatappi

1/4 cup (1/2 stick) unsalted butter

3 tablespoons all-purpose flour

3/4 cup half-and-half, warmed

1/2 cup heavy cream, warmed

2 teaspoons chopped fresh tarragon (substitute 1 teaspoon dried)

Pinch of freshly grated nutmeg

5 ounces Emmental, grated, divided

1/2 cup freshly grated Parmesan

4 ounces diced cooked chicken or turkey

Preheat the oven to 375°F. Grease a 13 x 9-inch baking pan. Have a bowl of ice water handy.

Place the stock in a saucepan and bring to a boil over high heat. Boil the stock until it is reduced by half. Set aside.

Bring a pot of salted water to a boil over high heat. Add the broccoli and cook for 3 to 4 minutes, or until crisp-tender. Remove the broccoli from the pot with a strainer and plunge it into the ice water to stop the cooking action.

Bring the water back to a boil. Cook the pasta until it is just beginning to soften to the al dente stage. Drain the pasta, run it under cold water, and return it to the pot. Drain the broccoli, and add it to the pot with the pasta.

Heat the butter in a saucepan over medium-low heat. Stir in the flour and cook, stirring constantly, for 1 minute, or until the mixture turns slightly beige, is bubbly, and appears to have grown in volume. Increase the heat to medium, and slowly whisk in the reduced stock, warm half-and-half, and warm cream. Bring to a boil, whisking frequently. Reduce the heat to low, stir in the tarragon and nutmeg, and simmer the sauce for 2 minutes.

Reserve 1/2 cup of the Emmental. Add the remaining cheese to the sauce by 1/2-cup measures, stirring until the cheese melts before making another addition. Pour the

Salt and freshly ground
    black pepper to taste
½ cup panko breadcrumbs

sauce over the pasta, add the chicken, and stir well. Season to taste with salt and pepper, and transfer the pasta to the prepared pan. Mix the reserved Emmental and breadcrumbs together, and sprinkle it over the top of the dish.

Bake the casserole for 20 to 30 minutes, or until the cheese sauce is bubbly and the crumbs on the top are deep brown. Allow to sit for 5 minutes, then serve.

Note: To prepare the dish in advance or reheat it, follow the instructions on page 26.

Variations:
• Substitute cauliflower or asparagus for the broccoli.
• Substitute Cheddar for both the Parmesan and Swiss cheeses.

TO AVOID THE HOUSE SMELLING LIKE BROCCOLI FOR A WEEK, add a piece of stale bread to the water in which it's boiling. The same is true for cauliflower, Brussels sprouts, and other members of the cabbage family. If you want to use this trick for this recipe, however, you'll have to bring another pot of water to a boil to cook the pasta.

MAYAN CHIPOTLE CHICKEN MAC AND CHEESE

Adapted from Macbar, New York, NY

With walls the color of bright orange Cheddar, this all-mac and cheese restaurant in New York's trendy SoHo is the creation of Chef Michael Ferraro, who also commands the kitchen at Delicatessen next door. Both spots offer whimsical comfort foods, with Macbar's offerings running the gamut from traditional four-cheeses to such innovations as this one made with spicy chicken and chiles.

MAKES 4 TO 6 SERVINGS

$^1/_2$ pound macaroni

$^1/_4$ cup ($^1/_2$ stick) unsalted butter

$^1/_4$ cup all-purpose flour

$2^1/_2$ cups whole milk, warmed

2 ounces Cheddar, grated

1 ounce fontina, grated

1 ounce American cheese, grated

2 ounces mascarpone

1 tablespoon olive oil

1 medium onion, diced, divided

3 garlic cloves, minced

3 chipotles in adobo sauce, pureed

$^1/_4$ cup freshly squeezed orange juice

(continued)

Preheat the oven to 375°F. Grease a 13 x 9-inch baking pan.

Bring a pot of salted water to a boil over high heat. Cook the pasta until it is just beginning to soften to the al dente stage. Drain the pasta, run it under cold water, and return it to the pot.

Heat the butter in a saucepan over medium-low heat. Stir in the flour and cook, stirring constantly, for 1 minute, or until the mixture turns slightly beige, is bubbly, and appears to have grown in volume. Increase the heat to medium, and slowly whisk in the warm milk. Bring to a boil, whisking frequently. Reduce the heat to low, and simmer the sauce for 2 minutes. Add the cheese to the sauce by $^1/_2$-cup measures, stirring until the cheese melts before making another addition.

Heat the oil in a medium skillet over medium heat. Add half of the onion and the garlic, and cook, stirring frequently, for 5 to 7 minutes, or until the onion is browned. Add the chiles, orange juice, chicken, cilantro, and oregano. Cook, stirring frequently, for 5 minutes, or until thickened.

(continued)

½ pound shredded cooked chicken

3 tablespoons chopped fresh cilantro

1 tablespoon chopped fresh oregano (substitute 1 teaspoon dried)

2 tablespoons freshly squeezed lime juice, or more to taste

Salt and freshly ground black pepper to taste

4 ounces Chihuahua cheese, grated

4 scallions, white parts and 4 inches of green tops, thinly sliced, for serving

Pour the sauce and chicken mixture over the pasta, and stir well. Stir in the lime juice, and season to taste with salt and pepper. Transfer the pasta to the prepared pan. Sprinkle the Chihuahua cheese over the top of the dish.

Bake the casserole for 20 to 30 minutes, or until the cheese sauce is bubbly and the crumbs on the top are deep brown. Allow to sit for 5 minutes, then serve, garnishing each serving with some sliced scallions.

Note: To prepare the dish in advance or reheat it, follow the instructions on page 26.

CHIPOTLES (PRONOUNCED CHEE-POOT-LAYS) ARE DRIED JALA-peño chiles that have then been smoked and then canned in a spicy sauce similar to a hot sauce. Unless you're making a huge batch, you'll use only a portion of a can in a given recipe. To save the remainder, place a few chiles with a teaspoon of sauce in ice cube trays. When they're frozen, transfer them to a heavy resealable plastic bag. Be sure to wash the ice cube tray well.

BUFFALO CHICKEN MAC AND CHEESE

Adapted from Rockit Bar and Grill, Chicago, IL

Chefs James Gottwald and Amanda Downing joined two favorite bar foods— mac and cheese and Buffalo chicken—for this delicious hybrid. There's Gorgonzola in the sauce, and if you serve some celery sticks on the side, the metaphor is complete.

MAKES 4 TO 6 SERVINGS

1/2 pound cavatappi

1 1/2 cups heavy cream

2 tablespoons freshly grated Parmesan cheese

1/4 cup firmly packed shredded Monterey Jack

1/4 cup crumbled Gorgonzola, divided

Salt and freshly ground black pepper to taste

2 tablespoons unsalted butter

1 to 2 tablespoons hot sauce, such as Frank's

2 teaspoons cider vinegar

1 large grilled or broiled boneless, skinless chicken breast, diced

2 tablespoons snipped fresh chives, for serving

Bring a pot of salted water to a boil over high heat. Cook the pasta until it is al dente. Drain the pasta, run it under cold water, and return it to the pot.

Bring the cream to a boil in a small saucepan, and cook over low heat until reduced by one quarter. Whisk in the Parmesan, Monterey Jack, and half of the Gorgonzola. Bring to a simmer, and cook for 1 minute. Season the sauce to taste with salt and pepper, and set aside.

Heat the butter, hot sauce, and vinegar in a small skillet. Add the chicken, and toss the cubes to coat them evenly with the sauce.

Add the sauce to the pasta, and stir well. Fold in the chicken, and season to taste with salt and pepper. Cook over low heat until the pasta is hot and coated with the sauce. Serve immediately, garnishing each serving with the remaining Gorgonzola and chives.

Note: The sauce and the chicken can be prepared up to 2 days in advance and refrigerated separately. Bring it to a simmer over low heat. Do not cook the pasta until just prior to serving.

BUFFALO WINGS WERE AN ACCIDENTAL CREATION OF TERESA Bellisimo, the mother of the owner of the Anchor Bar in Buffalo, NY. They were immortalized and the popularized when Calvin Trillin wrote about them in *The New Yorker* in the late 1970s.

MAC AND CHEESE WITH CHICKEN AND PROSCIUTTO

Chicken to a cook is like a blank canvas to a painter; it absorbs almost any seasoning and takes on myriad flavors excellently. In this dish it's sauced with a combination of two classic partners—Gruyère and Emmental—with some aromatic herbs and salty prosciutto thrown in for good measure.

MAKES 4 TO 6 SERVINGS

- $1/2$ pound rotini
- 6 tablespoons unsalted butter, divided
- 1 shallot, minced
- 1 garlic clove, minced
- 1 (4-ounce) boneless skinless chicken breast, cut into $3/4$-inch dice
- 1 tablespoon chopped fresh parsley
- 1 teaspoon fresh thyme (substitute $1/4$ teaspoon dried)
- Salt and freshly ground black pepper to taste
- 3 tablespoons all-purpose flour
- 2 cups whole milk, warmed
- 6 ounces Gruyère, grated
- 2 ounces Emmental, grated
- 3 ounces prosciutto, diced
- $1/2$ cup frozen peas, thawed
- $1/4$ cup freshly grated Parmesan
- $1/2$ cup panko breadcrumbs

Preheat the oven to 375°F. Grease a 13 x 9-inch baking pan.

Bring a pot of salted water to a boil over high heat. Cook the pasta until it is just beginning to soften to the al dente stage. Drain the pasta, run it under cold water, and return it to the pot.

Heat 2 tablespoons of the butter in a skillet over medium-high heat. Add the shallot and garlic, and cook, stirring frequently, for 2 minutes. Add the chicken, parsley, and thyme. Season to taste with salt and pepper. Cook for 3 to 4 minutes, or until the chicken is cooked through and no longer pink. Add the chicken mixture to the pot with the pasta.

Heat the remaining butter in a saucepan over medium-low heat. Stir in the flour and cook, stirring constantly, for 1 minute, or until the mixture turns slightly beige, is bubbly, and appears to have grown in volume. Increase the heat to medium, and slowly whisk in the warm milk. Bring to a boil, whisking frequently. Reduce the heat to low, and simmer the sauce for 2 minutes.

Add the cheese to the sauce by $1/2$-cup measures, stirring until the cheese melts before making another addition. Pour the sauce over the pasta, and stir well.

Stir in the prosciutto and peas, and season to taste with salt and pepper. Transfer the pasta to the prepared pan.

Mix the Parmesan and breadcrumbs together, and sprinkle it over the top of the dish.

Bake the casserole for 20 to 30 minutes, or until the cheese sauce is bubbly and the crumbs on the top are deep brown. Allow to sit for 5 minutes, then serve.

Note: To prepare the dish in advance or reheat it, follow the instructions on page 26.

THIS IS ACTUALLY A MAC AND CHEESE VARIATION ON CHICKEN cordon bleu, an entrée popular in the 1970s when I first starting having dinner parties. The dish had nothing to do with the respected cooking school in Paris, although the phrase *cordon bleu* had come to mean a dish cooked by a talented chef because the wearing of a blue ribbon (cordon bleu) related to a high order of knights created by French King Henri III in the late sixteenth century.

SHERRIED TURKEY AND MUSHROOM MAC AND CHEESE

This is an updated version of Turkey Tetrazzini, the grandmother of all left-over poultry casseroles. It was named for Italian singer Luisa Tetrazzini, who was the toast of the American opera circuit in the early 1900s. We don't know where or by whom the dish was invented.

MAKES 4 TO 6 SERVINGS

½ pound penne

¼ cup (½ stick) unsalted butter, divided

2 tablespoons olive oil

2 shallots, diced

2 garlic cloves, minced

1 celery rib, diced

4 ounces button mushrooms, wiped with a damp paper towel, trimmed, and sliced

Salt and freshly ground black pepper to taste

2 tablespoons all-purpose flour

⅓ cup dry sherry

1 cup half-and-half, warmed

¾ cup whole milk, warmed

3 ounces freshly grated Parmesan, divided

3 ounces whole-milk mozzarella, grated

½ cup shredded cooked turkey or chicken

½ cup plain breadcrumbs

Preheat the oven to 375°F. Grease a 13 x 9-inch baking pan.

Bring a pot of salted water to a boil over high heat. Cook the pasta until it is just beginning to soften to the al dente stage. Drain the pasta, run it under cold water, and return it to the pot.

Heat 2 tablespoons of the butter and the oil in a skillet over medium-high heat. Add the shallots, garlic, and celery. Cook, stirring frequently, for 3 minutes, or until the shallots are translucent. Add the mushrooms, and season to taste with salt and pepper. Cook for 5 to 7 minutes, or until the mushrooms soften and the liquid evaporates from the pan. Scrape the vegetable mixture into the pot with the pasta.

Heat the remaining butter in a saucepan over medium-low heat. Stir in the flour and cook, stirring constantly, for 1 minute, or until the mixture turns slightly beige, is bubbly, and appears to have grown in volume. Increase the heat to medium, and slowly whisk in the sherry. Cook for 2 minutes. Whisk in the warm half-and-half and milk. Bring to a boil, whisking frequently. Reduce the heat to low, and simmer the sauce for 2 minutes.

Reserve ½ cup of the Parmesan. Add the remaining Parmesan and the mozzarella to the sauce by ½-cup measures, stirring until the cheese melts before making another addition. Pour the sauce over the pasta, add the turkey, and stir well. Season to taste with salt and pepper, and transfer the pasta to the prepared pan. Mix the reserved Parmesan and breadcrumbs together, and sprinkle it over the top of the dish.

Bake the casserole for 20 to 30 minutes, or until the cheese sauce is bubbly and the crumbs on the top are deep brown. Allow to sit for 5 minutes, then serve.

Note: To prepare the dish in advance or reheat it, follow the instructions on page 26.

SHERRY IS A BRANDY-FORTIFIED WINE MADE FROM WHITE Palomino grapes grown near the town of Jerez in southern Spain. Sherry is the Anglicization of *Jerez*, and authentic sherry comes in a range of styles from bone dry to very sweet.

MAC QUACK WITH DUCK AND CARAMELIZED ONIONS

Adapted from Macbar, New York, NY

Macbar is one of the growing group of restaurants that features only mac and cheese variations on its menu. Located in New York's SoHo arts district, the small restaurant features plastic bowls in the shape of elbow macaroni for its carryout dishes. One of the unusual combinations created by Chef Michael Ferraro incorporates succulent duck meat and caramelized onions along with fresh thyme in the sauce.

MAKES 4 TO 6 SERVINGS

$^1/_2$ pound macaroni

$^1/_4$ cup ($^1/_2$ stick) unsalted butter, divided

2 tablespoons olive oil

1 large sweet onion, such as Vidalia or Bermuda, thinly sliced

Salt and freshly ground black pepper to taste

1 garlic clove, minced

1 teaspoon fresh thyme (substitute $^1/_4$ teaspoon dried)

$^1/_4$ cup all-purpose flour

$2^1/_2$ cups whole milk, warmed

4 ounces fontina, grated, divided

1 ounce American cheese, grated

2 ounces mascarpone

Preheat the oven to 375°F. Grease a 13 x 9-inch baking pan.

Bring a pot of salted water to a boil over high heat. Cook the pasta until it is just beginning to soften to the al dente stage. Drain the pasta, run it under cold water, and return it to the pot.

Melt 1 tablespoon of the butter and the oil in a skillet over medium heat. Add the onion, salt, and pepper, and toss to coat the onion. Cover the skillet, and cook for 5 minutes, stirring occasionally. Uncover the skillet, and cook over medium-high heat for 10 to 15 minutes, or until the onion is dark brown. Add the garlic and thyme, and cook for an additional 2 minutes. Set aside.

Heat the remaining butter in a saucepan over medium-low heat. Stir in the flour and cook, stirring constantly, for 1 minute, or until the mixture turns slightly beige, is bubbly, and appears to have grown in volume. Increase the heat to medium, and slowly whisk in the warm milk. Bring to a boil, whisking frequently. Reduce the heat to low, and simmer the sauce for 2 minutes.

Reserve $^3/_4$ cup of the fontina. Add the remaining

½ cup shredded cooked
   duck meat

1 scallion, white part and 4
   inches of green top,
   chopped

1 tablespoon chopped fresh
   chives

1 teaspoon freshly
   squeezed lemon juice

Dash of hot sauce

3 ounces Cheddar, grated

fontina, American cheese, and mascarpone to the sauce by ½-cup measures, stirring until the cheese melts before making another addition. Pour the sauce over the pasta, and stir well.

Stir in the onions, duck, scallions, chives, lemon juice, and hot sauce. Season to taste with salt and pepper, and transfer the pasta to the prepared pan. Mix the reserved fontina and Cheddar together, and sprinkle it over the top of the dish.

Bake the casserole for 20 to 30 minutes, or until the cheese sauce is bubbly and the crumbs on the top are deep brown. Allow to sit for 5 minutes, then serve.

Note: To prepare the dish in advance or reheat it, follow the instructions on page 26.

Variation:

• Substitute dark meat chicken for the duck. The flavor is not as rich as that of duck but it is close enough when folded in with all the other ingredients.

WHILE SPECIALTY FOOD COMPANIES LIKE D'ARTAGNAN SELL confit of duck online, and it's carried in some upscale supermarkets, the easiest way to get some cooked duck is at a Chinese restaurant. You can enjoy part of the Peking duck, including the delicious mahogany-colored skin, and you'll have plenty of meat for this dish.

CHEESEBURGER MAC AND CHEESE

Adapted from S'MAC, New York, NY

When Sarita and Caesar Ekya were thinking about the concept of S'MAC, the whole theme was to be comfort foods. And what could fit the definition better than a cheeseburger on a plate? While there's no pickle in Sarita's recipe, I usually put a few slices on top of my serving.

MAKES 4 TO 6 SERVINGS

¹/₂ pound macaroni

1 tablespoon olive oil

12 ounces lean ground beef

¹/₃ cup diced onion

2 garlic cloves, minced

1¹/₂ tablespoons Dijon mustard

1¹/₂ tablespoons ketchup

Salt and freshly ground black pepper to taste

1 tablespoon unsalted butter

1 tablespoon all-purpose flour

1 cup whole milk, warmed

4 ounces sharp yellow Cheddar, grated, divided

3 ounces American cheese, grated

¹/₄ cup plain breadcrumbs

Preheat the oven to 375°F. Grease a 13 x 9-inch baking pan.

Bring a pot of salted water to a boil over high heat. Cook the pasta until it is just beginning to soften to the al dente stage. Drain the pasta, run it under cold water, and return it to the pot.

Heat the oil in a skillet over medium-high heat. Crumble the beef into the skillet, and cook, breaking up lumps with a fork, for 2 to 3 minutes, or until browned. Remove the beef from the skillet with a slotted spoon, and discard the grease. Return the beef to the skillet, and add the onion, garlic, mustard, and ketchup. Cook over low heat, stirring frequently, for 3 to 5 minutes, or until the onion softens. Season to taste with salt and pepper, and set aside.

Heat the butter in a saucepan over medium-low heat. Stir in the flour and cook, stirring constantly, for 1 minute, or until the mixture turns slightly beige, is bubbly, and appears to have grown in volume. Increase the heat to medium, and slowly whisk in the warm milk. Bring to a boil, whisking frequently. Reduce the heat to low, and simmer the sauce for 2 minutes.

Reserve ³/₄ cup of the Cheddar. Add the remaining Cheddar and the American cheese to the sauce by ¹/₂-cup measures, stirring until the cheese melts before making another addition.

Pour the sauce and hamburger mixture over the pasta, and stir well. Season to taste with salt and pepper, and transfer the pasta to the prepared pan. Mix the reserved Cheddar and breadcrumbs together, and sprinkle it over the top of the dish.

Bake the casserole for 20 to 30 minutes, or until the cheese sauce is bubbly and the crumbs on the top are deep brown. Allow to sit for 5 minutes, then serve.

Note: To prepare the dish in advance or reheat it, follow the instructions on page 26.

CHEDDAR IS NATURALLY A BEIGE CHEESE, AND THE ORANGE color is a dye made from annatto seed. Cheese historians say that when cows graze on fresh grass there is more beta-carotene in their milk, and the cheese produced during the summer months has more color than when the cows are eating hay in the winter months. While these cheeses might have a blush of orange, the pumpkin tone we associate with Cheddar is a dye.

PHILLY CHEESESTEAK MAC AND CHEESE

Adapted from Cheese-ology, St. Louis, MO

The combination of thinly sliced beef with sautéed onions and peppers smothered in an American cheese sauce has become a national favorite, right up there with the cheeseburger. Here is the mac and cheese version.

MAKES 4 TO 6 SERVINGS

8 ounces flank steak or sirloin tip

2 tablespoons olive oil

1/2 green bell pepper, seeds and ribs removed, chopped

1/2 small onion, chopped

Salt and freshly ground black pepper to taste

1/2 pound macaroni

1/4 cup (1/2 stick) unsalted butter

1/4 cup all-purpose flour

2 cups whole milk, warmed

1/4 teaspoon freshly grated nutmeg

4 ounces white American cheese, grated

3 ounces mild provolone, grated

1/2 cup panko breadcrumbs

Place the steak on a sheet of plastic wrap, and place it in the freezer for 20 to 30 minutes, or until it is partially frozen and stiff. Slice the beef against the grain into slices 1/4-inch thick and 1/2-inch wide.

Heat the oil in a skillet over medium heat. Add the green pepper and onion, and cook, stirring frequently, for 5 to 7 minutes, or until the vegetables soften. Add the sliced beef, and season it to taste with salt and pepper. Sauté the beef for 1 minute, or until lightly browned. Set aside.

Preheat the oven to 375°F. Grease a 13 x 9-inch baking pan.

Bring a pot of salted water to a boil over high heat. Cook the pasta until it is just beginning to soften to the al dente stage. Drain the pasta, run it under cold water, and return it to the pot.

Heat the butter in a saucepan over medium-low heat. Stir in the flour and cook, stirring constantly, for 1 minute, or until the mixture turns slightly beige, is bubbly, and appears to have grown in volume. Increase the heat to medium, and slowly whisk in the warm milk. Bring to a boil, whisking frequently. Reduce the heat to low, stir in the nutmeg, and simmer the sauce for 2 minutes.

Add the cheese to the sauce by 1/2-cup measures, stirring until the cheese melts before making another addition.

Pour the sauce over the pasta, and stir well. Fold in the beef mixture, season to taste with salt and pepper, and transfer the pasta to the prepared pan. Sprinkle the breadcrumbs on top of the dish.

Bake the casserole for 20 to 30 minutes, or until the cheese sauce is bubbly and the crumbs on the top are deep brown. Allow to sit for 5 minutes, then serve.

Note: To prepare the dish in advance or reheat it, follow the instructions on page 26.

BLACK AND BLEU MAC AND CHEESE

Adapted from Cheese-ology, St. Louis, MO

Placing crumbles of blue cheese on top of steak has been popular for decades. The sharpness of the cheese serves as a foil to the richness of the meat. The same is true for this mac and cheese version, given some spice with Cajun seasoning.

MAKES 4 TO 6 SERVINGS

- 8 ounces flank steak or sirloin tip
- 2 tablespoons olive oil
- 1 teaspoon Cajun seasoning or to taste
- $1/2$ pound macaroni
- $1/4$ cup ($1/2$ stick) unsalted butter
- $1/4$ cup all-purpose flour
- 2 cups whole milk, warmed
- $1/4$ teaspoon freshly grated nutmeg
- 4 ounces white American cheese, grated
- 3 ounces crumbled bleu cheese
- Salt and freshly ground black pepper to taste
- $1/2$ cup panko breadcrumbs

Place the steak on a sheet of plastic wrap, and place it in the freezer for 20 to 30 minutes, or until it is partially frozen and stiff. Slice the beef against the grain into slices $1/2$-inch thick and $1/2$-inch wide. Heat the oil in a skillet over medium-high heat. Add the beef, and sprinkle it with the Cajun seasoning. Sauté the beef for 1 minute, or until lightly browned. Set aside.

Preheat the oven to 375°F. Grease a 13 x 9-inch baking pan. Bring a pot of salted water to a boil over high heat. Cook the pasta until it is just beginning to soften to the al dente stage. Drain the pasta, run it under cold water, and return it to the pot.

Heat the butter in a saucepan over medium-low heat. Stir in the flour and cook, stirring constantly, for 1 minute, or until the mixture turns slightly beige, is bubbly, and appears to have grown in volume. Increase the heat to medium, and slowly whisk in the warm milk. Bring to a boil, whisking frequently. Reduce the heat to low, stir in the nutmeg, and simmer the sauce for 2 minutes.

Add the cheese to the sauce by $1/2$-cup measures, stirring until the cheese melts before making another addition. Pour the sauce over the pasta, and add the cooked beef.

Stir well, season to taste with salt and pepper, and transfer the pasta to the prepared pan. Sprinkle the breadcrumbs on top of the dish.

Bake the casserole for 20 to 30 minutes, or until the cheese sauce is bubbly and the crumbs on the top are deep brown. Allow to sit for 5 minutes, then serve.

Note: To prepare the dish in advance or reheat it, follow the instructions on page 26.

AMERICAN CHEESE WAS DEVELOPED IN THE NINETEENTH CEN-tury and is mentioned in Dickens's journals when he visited the US. During World War II the government imposed restrictions on cheese consumption as a rationing measure. American cheese was the only one allowed to be sold, due to its abundance and the scarcity of imported cheeses. The ban was imposed in May of 1942, but rescinded three months later due to public outcry on both sides of the Atlantic.

PASTITSIO-STYLE MAC AND CHEESE

Pastitsio is a traditional Greek mac and cheese. What differentiates it from similar casseroles is that it's baked in two layers. The bottom pasta is sauced with a mixture of spiced lamb and tomatoes, and the cheese sauce on top is made primarily with sharp feta.

MAKES 4 TO 6 SERVINGS

1/2 pound small penne

2 tablespoons olive oil

1 medium onion, diced

2 garlic cloves, minced

12 ounces ground lamb

1 tablespoon chopped fresh oregano (substitute 1 teaspoon dried)

1/4 teaspoon ground cinnamon

1/2 cup dry red wine

1 (14.5-ounce) can petite diced tomatoes, undrained

1 (8-ounce) can tomato sauce

Salt and freshly ground black pepper to taste

2 tablespoons unsalted butter

3 tablespoons all-purpose flour

Preheat the oven to 375°F. Grease a 13 x 9-inch baking pan.

Bring a pot of salted water to a boil over high heat. Cook the pasta until it is just beginning to soften to the al dente stage. Drain the pasta, run it under cold water, and return it to the pot.

Heat the oil in a large skillet over medium-high heat. Add the onion and garlic, and cook, stirring frequently, for 3 minutes, or until the onion is translucent. Crumble the lamb into the skillet, and cook, breaking up lumps with a fork, for 3 minutes, or until the lamb is browned. Stir in the oregano, cinnamon, and wine. Cook, stirring frequently, for 5 minutes, or until the wine is reduced by half. Add the tomatoes and tomato sauce, reduce the heat to low, and simmer the lamb sauce, uncovered, for 30 minutes, or until thickened.

Stir half of the pasta into the lamb sauce, season to taste with salt and pepper, and transfer the pasta to the prepared pan.

Heat the butter in a saucepan over medium-low heat. Stir in the flour and cook, stirring constantly, for 1 minute, or until the mixture turns slightly beige, is bubbly, and appears to have grown in volume. Increase the heat to

1 1/2 cups whole milk, warmed

6 ounces crumbled feta

2 ounces fontina, grated

2 large eggs, lightly beaten

1 ounce freshly grated Parmesan

1/2 cup panko breadcrumbs

medium, and slowly whisk in the warm milk. Bring to a boil, whisking frequently. Reduce the heat to low, and simmer the sauce for 2 minutes.

Add the cheese to the sauce by 1/2-cup measures, stirring until the cheese melts before making another addition. Pour the sauce over the remaining pasta, and stir well. Stir in the eggs, and season to taste with salt and pepper.

Layer the cheese pasta on top of the lamb mixture. Combine the Parmesan and breadcrumbs, and sprinkle it on top of the dish.

Bake the casserole for 20 to 30 minutes, or until the cheese sauce is bubbly and the crumbs on the top are deep brown. Allow to sit for 5 minutes, then serve.

Note: To prepare the dish in advance or reheat it, follow the instructions on page 26.

Variations:

- Substitute ground beef for the lamb.
- Substitute 1 (1-pound) eggplant, cut into 3/4-inch cubes, for the lamb. Soak the eggplant in salted water for 20 minutes. Wring it dry in a cloth tea towel, and then sauté it in place of the meat.

SPICY LINGUIÇA MAC AND CHEESE

Many European cuisines have their own versions of mac and cheese, and this one is based on a dish I ate in Portugal a few years ago. The spiciness comes from both the sausage and the cheese, and aromatic smoked paprika adds another layer of flavor.

MAKES 4 TO 6 SERVINGS

- ½ pound gemelli
- 6 ounces bulk linguiça sausage (substitute link sausage with the casings discarded)
- 1 medium onion, diced
- 2 garlic cloves, minced
- ½ red bell pepper, seeds and ribs removed, diced
- 2 tablespoons smoked Spanish paprika
- ½ teaspoon dried oregano
- ¾ cup chicken stock
- 2 tablespoons unsalted butter
- 2 tablespoons all-purpose flour
- 1½ cups half-and-half, warmed
- 4 ounces Manchego, grated
- 2 ounces jalapeño Jack, grated
- Salt and freshly ground black pepper to taste

Bring a pot of salted water to a boil over high heat. Cook the pasta until it is al dente. Drain the pasta, run it under cold water, and return it to the pot.

Heat a medium skillet over medium-high heat. Crumble the linguiça into the skillet, and cook, stirring frequently, for 3 to 4 minutes, or until the sausage is browned. Add the onion, garlic, and red pepper to the skillet, and cook, stirring frequently, for 3 minutes, or until the onion is translucent. Stir in the paprika and oregano, and cook for 1 minute, stirring constantly. Add the stock, stir well, and bring to a boil. Reduce the heat to medium, and cook the mixture for 5 minutes, or until the vegetables soften and the liquid is reduced by half. Set aside.

Heat the butter in a saucepan over medium-low heat. Stir in the flour and cook, stirring constantly, for 1 minute, or until the mixture turns slightly beige, is bubbly, and appears to have grown in volume. Increase the heat to medium, and slowly whisk in the warm milk. Bring to a boil, whisking frequently. Reduce the heat to low, and simmer the sauce for 2 minutes.

Add the cheese to the sauce by ½-cup measures, stirring until the cheese melts before making another addition.

Add the sauce to the pasta, stir in the sausage mixture, and season to taste with salt and pepper. Cook over low heat until the pasta is hot and coated with the sauce. Serve immediately.

Note: The sauce and sausage mixture can be prepared up to 2 days in advance and refrigerated. Bring it to a simmer over low heat. Do not cook the pasta until just prior to serving.

IT'S EASIER TO SLICE AND DICE BELL PEPPERS FROM THE INSIDE out. Once the seeds and ribs have been removed, place the peppers skin-side down on your cutting board, and you'll find it's easier to control your knife and cut the size pieces you desire.

PORKY MACS

The most popular addition to mac and cheese on restaurant menus around the country is some type of cured or smoked pork, especially bacon and prosciutto. The earthy and salty food creates a yin-yang with creamy cheeses of all types.

While it's difficult to find a broad range of types of prosciutto in American markets, the quality of the bacon you use makes as much a difference in the finished dish as the quality of the cheeses in the sauce. Select bacon from small smokehouses, rather than national or supermarket brands.

A way to personalize these dishes is by selecting a type of bacon that suits your personal taste. Some bacons are smoked over hickory wood, while others are smoked over oak or maple. They vary greatly in terms of sweetness and saltiness, so it is important to choose the bacon that both pleases your palate and is right for the dish.

ALPINE MAC AND CHEESE WITH BACON AND GRUYÈRE

Adapted from S'MAC, New York, NY

This mac and cheese is a wonderful brunch dish; it's flavored like a classic quiche Lorraine with lots of nutty Gruyère and some mellow Muenster included in the sauce.

MAKES 4 TO 6 SERVINGS

$^1/_2$ pound macaroni

8 ounces thick-sliced bacon, cut into $^1/_2$-inch pieces

2 tablespoons unsalted butter

2 tablespoons all-purpose flour

$1^1/_2$ cups whole milk, warmed

$1^1/_2$ teaspoons Worcestershire sauce

6 ounces Gruyère, grated

2 ounces Muenster, grated

Salt and freshly ground black pepper to taste

3 ounces provolone, grated

$^1/_4$ cup plain breadcrumbs

Preheat the oven to 375°F. Grease a 13 x 9-inch baking pan.

Bring a pot of salted water to a boil over high heat. Cook the pasta until it is just beginning to soften to the al dente stage. Drain the pasta, run it under cold water, and return it to the pot.

Place the bacon in a skillet and cook over medium-high heat, stirring occasionally, for 5 to 7 minutes, or until the bacon is crisp. Remove the bacon from the pan with a slotted spoon, and drain on paper towels. Reserve 1 tablespoon of the bacon grease.

Heat the butter in a saucepan over medium-low heat. Stir in the flour and cook, stirring constantly, for 1 minute, or until the mixture turns slightly beige, is bubbly, and appears to have grown in volume. Increase the heat to medium, and slowly whisk in the warm milk. Bring to a boil, whisking frequently. Reduce the heat to low, stir in the Worcestershire sauce, and simmer the sauce for 2 minutes.

Add the cheese to the sauce by $^1/_2$-cup measures, stirring until the cheese melts before making another addition. Add the bacon and bacon grease to the pasta. Pour the sauce over the pasta, and stir well. Season to taste with salt and pepper, and transfer the pasta to the prepared pan. Combine the provolone and breadcrumbs, and sprinkle the mixture on top of the dish.

Bake the casserole for 20 to 30 minutes, or until the cheese sauce is bubbly and the crumbs on the top are deep brown. Allow to sit for 5 minutes, then serve.

Note: To prepare the dish in advance or reheat it, follow the instructions on page 26.

NEVER DISPOSE OF BACON GREASE BY POURING IT DOWN THE drain. It can easily clog up the pipes. Wash out empty heavy-duty cardboard containers from half-and-half or heavy cream and save them under the sink. Pour the bacon grease into one, and once it's cooled, dispose of it with your trash. Better yet, pour cooled grease into glass jars to save in your refrigerator; use it in place of olive oil or butter for a smokier flavor.

MAC AND CHEESE WITH BACON AND FOUR CHEESES

Adapted from The Tipsy Pig, San Francisco, CA

Michael Bauer, the food editor for *The San Francisco Chronicle*, proclaimed that the mac and cheese he had at Chef Sam Josi's gastropub was the best he'd ever eaten, and once you try this recipe you'll know why. Opened in 2009, The Tipsy Pig is a hip and swinging restaurant that offers comfort food created with care. The mac and cheese is actually finished off with a bit of bacon grease, and the combination of cheeses in the sauce is superb.

MAKES 4 TO 6 SERVINGS

1/2 pound ditalini

1 tablespoon olive oil

2 ounces thick bacon, diced

2 tablespoons unsalted butter

2 tablespoons all-purpose flour

1 1/2 cups heavy cream, warmed

3 ounces white Cheddar, grated

3 ounces Gouda, grated

1 tablespoon crumbled blue cheese

Salt and freshly ground white pepper to taste

1 ounce freshly grated Parmesan, for serving

3 tablespoons chopped fresh parsley, for serving

Bring a pot of salted water to a boil over high heat. Cook the pasta until it is al dente. Drain the pasta, run it under cold water, and return it to the pot. Toss it with the olive oil.

Cook the bacon in a skillet over medium-high heat for 5 to 7 minutes, or until crisp. Remove the bacon from the pan with a slotted spoon, and drain on paper towels. Set aside. Reserve 3 tablespoons of the bacon grease for finishing the dish.

Heat the butter in a saucepan over medium-low heat. Stir in the flour and cook, stirring constantly, for 1 minute, or until the mixture turns slightly beige, is bubbly, and appears to have grown in volume. Increase the heat to medium, and slowly whisk in the cream. Bring to a boil, whisking frequently. Reduce the heat to low, and simmer the sauce for 2 minutes.

Add the Cheddar and Gouda to the sauce by 1/2-cup measures, stirring until the cheese melts before making another addition. Stir in the blue cheese. Add the bacon, reserved bacon grease, and sauce to the pasta, and season to taste with salt and pepper. Cook over low heat until the pasta is hot and coated with the sauce.

Serve immediately, sprinkling each serving with Parmesan and parsley.

Note: The sauce can be prepared up to 2 days in advance and refrigerated. Bring it to a simmer over low heat. Do not cook the pasta until just prior to serving.

AN ALTERNATIVE TO FRYING BACON IS TO BAKE IT ON A RACK set on a rimmed sheet pan in a 375°F oven until crisp. The length of time will depend on the thickness of the bacon, but count on at least 20 minutes.

BACON AND CHEDDAR MAC AND CHEESE WITH SCALLIONS AND SOUR CREAM

Adapted from Mother's Bistro & Bar, Portland, OR

When Lisa Schroeder was a young mother about twenty years ago, there were few restaurants featuring the sort of comforting "mother food" she craved. She entered the Culinary Institute of America, where she graduated with honors in 1995 and then worked in legendary kitchens such as Lespinasse in New York and at Roger Vergé's Moulin de Mougins in France. In 2000 her dream was realized when she opened Mother's Bistro & Bar.

MAKES 4 TO 6 SERVINGS

$\frac{1}{2}$ pound fusilli

5 ounces bacon, diced

1$\frac{1}{2}$ cups heavy cream

4 ounces sharp Cheddar, grated

Salt and freshly ground black pepper to taste

$\frac{1}{3}$ cup sour cream, for serving

3 scallions, white parts and 3 inches of green tops, thinly sliced, for serving

Bring a pot of salted water to a boil over high heat. Cook the pasta until it is al dente. Drain the pasta, and return it to the pot.

Cook the bacon in a skillet over medium-high heat for 5 to 7 minutes, or until crisp. Remove the bacon from the pan with a slotted spoon, and drain on paper towels. Set aside.

Discard the bacon grease from the skillet. Add the cream to the skillet, and bring to a boil over medium heat, stirring frequently. Stir the cream to incorporate the browned bits from the bottom of the skillet. Reduce the heat to low, and simmer the sauce for 5 minutes, or until slightly reduced. Add the cheese to the sauce by $\frac{1}{2}$-cup measures, stirring until the cheese melts before making another addition.

Add the sauce to the pasta, stir in the bacon, and season to taste with salt and pepper. Cook over low heat until the pasta is hot and coated with the sauce. Serve immediately, garnishing each portion with sour cream and scallions.

Note: The sauce can be prepared up to 2 days in advance and refrigerated. Bring it to a simmer over low heat. Do not cook the pasta until just prior to serving.

THE BROWN BITS THAT ARE STUCK TO ANY PAN IN WHICH PROTEIN is cooked are treasure troves of flavor, and they become the basis for pan sauces of all types. Every type of meat and poultry give off these bits of protein, which should always be incorporated to intensify the flavor of a sauce.

MAC AND GREENS

Adapted from Red Rooster Harlem, New York, NY

Named for a legendary speakeasy, Red Rooster Harlem is the brainchild of internationally renowned chef Marcus Samuelsson, who was born in Ethiopia, raised in Sweden, and was the chef who commanded the kitchen at Aquavit for more than a decade. He served as guest chef at the first State Dinner hosted by President Barack Obama, and is also the author of a number of acclaimed cookbooks. His version of mac and cheese is done with bacon and stewed collard greens, reflecting the American menu at Red Rooster Harlem.

MAKES 4 TO 6 SERVINGS

Greens

3 slices bacon

$1/4$ cup light coconut milk

2 tablespoons soy sauce

$1 1/2$ teaspoons grainy mustard

2 tablespoons olive oil

2 garlic cloves, halved

2 cups firmly packed shredded collard greens

2 cups shredded bok choy

Topping

$1/4$ cup panko breadcrumbs

$1/4$ cup toasted plain breadcrumbs

$1/4$ cup chopped fresh parsley

2 tablespoons freshly grated Parmesan

Salt and freshly ground white pepper to taste

(continued)

For the greens, cook the bacon in a large skillet over medium-high heat for 5 to 6 minutes, or until crisp. Remove the bacon from the pan, reserving the bacon grease. Drain the bacon on paper towels. Crumble the bacon, and set aside.

Combine the coconut milk and soy sauce in a small pan, and bring to a boil over medium heat. Stir in the mustard and bacon, and set aside.

Heat the olive oil and bacon grease over medium-low heat. Add the garlic and cook for 4 to 5 minutes, or until the garlic is pale golden. Remove and discard the garlic.

Raise the heat to medium-high, and add the collard greens. Cook, stirring frequently, until the greens wilt. Add the coconut milk mixture, cover the pan, and cook the greens over low heat for about 12 minutes, stirring occasionally, or until the greens are almost tender and the sauce has thickened. Add the bok choy, and cook, covered, for an additional 3 to 5 minutes, or until the tender. Set aside.

For the topping, combine the panko, breadcrumbs, parsley, Parmesan, salt, and pepper in a food processor fitted

(continued)

Pasta

- $1/2$ pound orecchiette
- $1/4$ cup ($1/2$ stick) unsalted butter
- 2 shallots, thinly sliced
- 1 tablespoon all-purpose flour
- 1 garlic clove, minced
- 2 cups heavy cream, warmed
- $1/2$ cup whole milk, warmed
- 4 ounces Cheddar, grated
- 2 ounces freshly grated Parmesan
- 2 ounces Gruyère, grated
- $1/2$ teaspoon freshly grated nutmeg
- $1/2$ teaspoon dry mustard powder
- Salt and freshly ground white pepper to taste

with the steel blade, and grind until fine using on-and-off pulsing. Set aside.

For the dish, preheat the oven to 375°F. Grease a 13 x 9-inch baking pan.

Bring a pot of salted water to a boil over high heat. Cook the pasta until it is just beginning to soften to the al dente stage. Drain the pasta, run it under cold water, and return it to the pot.

Heat the butter in a saucepan over medium-low heat. Add the shallots and cook for 7 to 10 minutes, or until the shallots are golden. Stir in the flour and garlic, and cook, stirring constantly, for 1 minute, or until the mixture turns slightly beige, is bubbly, and appears to have grown in volume. Increase the heat to medium, and slowly whisk in the warm cream and milk. Bring to a boil, whisking frequently. Reduce the heat to low, and simmer the sauce for 2 minutes.

Add the cheeses to the sauce by $1/2$-cup measures, stirring until the cheese melts before making another addition. Stir in the nutmeg and mustard.

Pour the sauce over the pasta, and stir well. Fold in the cooked greens, and season to taste with salt and pepper. Transfer the pasta to the prepared pan, and sprinkle the topping on top of the dish.

Bake the casserole for 20 to 30 minutes, or until the cheese sauce is bubbly and the crumbs on the top are deep brown. Allow to sit for 5 minutes, then serve.

Note: To prepare the dish in advance or reheat it, follow the instructions on page 26.

UNLIKE THE DIFFERENCE BETWEEN SKIM MILK AND WHOLE milk, there's virtually no difference in taste and texture between light coconut milk and regular coconut milk. What is different is the amount of fat, most of it saturated. Use light coconut milk whenever possible to keep foods healthful.

FRENCH ONION AND BACON MAC AND CHEESE

Adapted from MacDaddy's Macaroni & Cheese Bar, Monroe, CT

The combination of caramelized onions with salty bacon and nutty Gruyère makes this a wonderful side to serve with hearty roast chicken or pork loin.

MAKES 4 TO 6 SERVINGS

5 tablespoons unsalted butter, divided

1 tablespoon olive oil

1 medium onion, diced

1/2 teaspoon granulated sugar

Salt and freshly ground black pepper to taste

1/2 pound macaroni

3 tablespoons all-purpose flour

2 cups whole milk, warmed

3 ounces Gruyère, grated

1/2 cup crumbled cooked bacon

1 tablespoon heavy cream

Melt 1 tablespoon of the butter and the oil in a skillet over medium heat. Add the onion, sugar, salt, and pepper, and toss to coat. Cover, and cook for 5 minutes, stirring occasionally. Uncover, and cook over medium-high for 10 to 15 minutes, or until the onion is browned.

Bring a pot of salted water to a boil over high heat. Cook the pasta until it is al dente. Drain the pasta, run it under cold water, and return it to the pot.

Heat the remaining butter in a saucepan over medium-low heat. Stir in the flour and cook, stirring constantly, for 1 minute, or until the mixture turns slightly beige, is bubbly, and appears to have grown in volume. Increase the heat to medium, and slowly whisk in the warm milk. Bring to a boil, whisking frequently. Reduce the heat to low, and simmer the sauce for 2 minutes.

Add the cheese to the sauce by 1/2-cup measures, stirring until the cheese melts before making another addition. Stir the onion, bacon, and cream, and bring to a simmer.

Add the sauce to the pasta, and season to taste with salt and pepper. Cook over low heat until the pasta is hot and coated with the sauce. Serve immediately.

Note: The sauce can be prepared up to 2 days in advance and refrigerated, but don't add the bacon at that point. Bring it to a simmer over low heat, and stir in the bacon. Do not cook the pasta until just prior to serving.

BACON, TOMATO, AND CARAMELIZED ONION MAC AND CHEESE

Adapted from Wilde Bar & Restaurant, Chicago, IL

Wilde Bar & Restaurant, named for author Oscar Wilde, is an upscale Irish pub run by the Munster Tavern Group. The clubby atmosphere of the bar with working fireplaces, dark wooden walls, and a fireplace, attracts a loyal group of customers. Henry Pariser is executive chef for the group, which also includes Lady Gregory's, and his version of bacon mac and cheese includes tomatoes and caramelized onions.

MAKES 4 TO 6 SERVINGS

- 2 tablespoons unsalted butter, divided
- 3 tablespoons olive oil, divided
- 1 medium onion, diced
- 1 teaspoon granulated sugar
- Salt and freshly ground black pepper to taste
- ½ pound cavatappi
- 4 ounces bacon
- 4 garlic cloves, minced, divided
- 2 cups heavy cream
- 12 ounces Irish Cheddar, grated
- 1 ounce freshly grated Parmesan

Melt 1 tablespoon of the butter and 2 tablespoons of the oil in a skillet over medium heat. Add the onion, sugar, salt, and pepper, and toss to coat the onion. Cover the skillet, and cook for 5 minutes, stirring occasionally. Uncover the skillet, and cook over medium-high heat for 10 to 15 minutes, or until the onion is dark brown.

Preheat the oven to 375°F. Grease a 13 x 9-inch baking pan.

Bring a pot of salted water to a boil over high heat. Cook the pasta until it is just beginning to soften to the al dente stage. Drain the pasta, run it under cold water, and return it to the pot.

Cook the bacon in a skillet over medium-high heat for 5 to 7 minutes, or until crisp. Remove the bacon from the pan with a slotted spoon, and drain on paper towels. Crumble the bacon, and set aside.

Heat the remaining oil in a saucepan over medium heat. Add three-quarters of the garlic, and cook, stirring frequently, for 1 minute. Whisk in the cream. Bring to a boil, whisking frequently. Reduce the heat to low, and

3 ripe plum tomatoes,
  cored, seeded, and diced
$3/4$ cup panko breadcrumbs
1 tablespoon chopped
  fresh parsley

simmer the sauce for 2 minutes. Add the cheese to the sauce by $1/2$-cup measures, stirring until the cheese melts before making another addition.

Pour the sauce over the pasta, and stir well. Add the bacon and tomato, season to taste with salt and pepper, and transfer the pasta to the prepared pan. Melt the remaining butter, mix it with the remaining garlic, bread-crumbs, and parsley. Sprinkle it over the top of the dish.

Bake the casserole for 20 to 30 minutes, or until the cheese sauce is bubbly and the crumbs on the top are deep brown. Allow to sit for 5 minutes, then serve.

Note: To prepare the dish in advance or reheat it, follow the instructions on page 26.

AS GARLIC BECOMES OLD, BITTER GREEN SHOOTS BEGIN TO emergefrom the individual cloves. Never buy a head if the shoots are visible, but if you discover when you peel a clove that there is one, discard the green shoot before chopping or mincing the clove.

MAC ATTACK WITH BACON, CHEDDAR, AND APPLE

Adapted from Straw, San Francisco, CA

The whole premise of Straw is carnival fare. It's all lighthearted fun, from the old children's book covers on the menus to the tilt-a-whirl booths. Run by chef Naomi Beck, Straw opened in the Hayes Valley neighborhood in 2011. Her version of mac and cheese includes maple-glazed bacon and is topped with some crunchy fresh apple.

MAKES 4 TO 6 SERVINGS

$^1\!/_2$ pound macaroni

4 slices thick-cut bacon

1 tablespoon pure maple syrup

$^1\!/_4$ cup ($^1\!/_2$ stick) unsalted butter

$^1\!/_4$ cup all-purpose flour

1 teaspoon fresh thyme (substitute $^1\!/_4$ teaspoon dried)

2 cups heavy cream, warmed

12 ounces orange Cheddar, grated

1 tablespoon freshly squeezed lemon juice

$^1\!/_2$ teaspoon freshly grated nutmeg

Salt and freshly ground black pepper to taste

1 Red Delicious apple, cored and chopped

Bring a pot of salted water to a boil over high heat. Cook the pasta until it is al dente. Drain the pasta, run it under cold water, and return it to the pot.

Cook the bacon in a skillet over medium-high heat for 5 to 7 minutes, or until crisp. Remove the bacon from the pan with a slotted spoon, and drain on paper towels. Brush the maple syrup on the drained bacon. When cooled, crumble the bacon, and set aside.

Heat the butter in a saucepan over medium-low heat. Stir in the flour and thyme and cook, stirring constantly, for 1 minute, or until the mixture turns slightly beige, is bubbly, and appears to have grown in volume. Increase the heat to medium, and slowly whisk in the cream. Bring to a boil, whisking frequently. Reduce the heat to low, and simmer for 2 minutes. Add the cheese to the sauce by $^1\!/_2$-cup measures, stirring until it melts before making another addition. Stir in the lemon juice and nutmeg.

Add the sauce to the pasta, stir in the bacon, and season to taste with salt and pepper. Cook over low heat until the pasta is hot and coated with the sauce. Serve immediately, garnishing each serving with apple.

Note: The sauce can be prepared up to 2 days in advance and refrigerated. Bring it to a simmer over low heat. Do not cook the pasta until just prior to serving.

HAM AND GOAT CHEDDAR MAC AND CHEESE

Adapted from Vidalia, Washington, D.C.

Jeff Buben and his wife, Sallie, opened up this flagship for New American cuisine in the nation's capital in the early 1990s, and there has always been some version of mac and cheese as a side dish. This one, containing goat Cheddar, fresh goat curds, and country ham from nearby Virginia, has become a signature.

MAKES 4 TO 6 SERVINGS

$\frac{1}{2}$ pound macaroni

2 tablespoons unsalted butter

$\frac{1}{2}$ cup diced onion

2 garlic cloves, minced

$\frac{1}{4}$ cup all-purpose flour

2 cups heavy cream, warmed

1 cup half-and-half, warmed

1 bay leaf

1 teaspoon chopped fresh thyme (substitute pinch dried)

1 teaspoon chopped fresh rosemary (substitute $\frac{1}{2}$ teaspoon dried)

1 teaspoon mustard powder

1 teaspoon freshly grated nutmeg

Preheat the oven to 375°F. Grease a 13 x 9-inch baking pan.

Bring a pot of salted water to a boil over high heat. Cook the pasta until it is just beginning to soften to the al dente stage. Drain the pasta, run it under cold water, and return it to the pot.

Heat the butter in a saucepan over medium-low heat. Add the onion and garlic and cook, stirring frequently, for 3 minutes, or until the onion is translucent. Stir in the flour and cook, stirring constantly, for 1 minute, or until the mixture turns slightly beige, is bubbly, and appears to have grown in volume. Increase the heat to medium, and slowly whisk in the warm cream and half-and-half. Bring to a boil, whisking frequently. Stir in the bay leaf, thyme, rosemary, mustard, and nutmeg. Reduce the heat to low, and simmer the sauce for 2 minutes.

Reserve $\frac{1}{2}$ cup of the Cheddar. Add the remaining Cheddar and goat cheese curds to the sauce by $\frac{1}{2}$-cup measures, stirring until the cheese melts before making another addition. Remove and discard the bay leaf. Pour the sauce over the pasta, and stir well. Stir in the ham and

3 ounces cave-aged goat Cheddar (substitute any sharp white Cheddar), grated, divided

2 ounces goat cheese curds

2 ounces country ham, chopped

Salt and freshly ground black pepper to taste

½ cup Ritz cracker crumbs

reserved cheese. Season to taste with salt and pepper, and transfer the pasta to the prepared pan. Sprinkle the crumbs over the top of the dish.

Bake the casserole for 20 to 30 minutes, or until the cheese sauce is bubbly and the crumbs on the top are deep brown. Allow to sit for 5 minutes, then serve.

Note: To prepare the dish in advance or reheat it, follow the instructions on page 26.

THE NUTMEG TREE IS A TROPICAL EVERGREEN NATIVE TO Indonesia, and nutmeg has been one of the most prized spices throughout history. Arab merchants brought it to Constantinople in the sixth century, and control over Europe's supply of nutmeg led to wars between the English and Dutch. Nutmeg and mace come from the same tree. Nutmeg is the seed and mace is the lacy covering around the seed.

MAC AND CHEESE SOUFFLÉ WITH COUNTRY HAM

Adapted from Sweet Potatoes, Winston-Salem, NC

Chef Stephanie Tyson and her business partner, Vivián Joyner, opened up Sweet Potatoes Restaurant in the Downtown Arts District of Winston-Salem in 2003, and there's nothing frou-frou about their food; it's Southern cooking at its best. Her version of mac and cheese contains a mix of three cheeses, plus the great taste of country ham.

MAKES 4 TO 6 SERVINGS

¹/₂ pound macaroni

4 ounces sharp Cheddar, grated, divided

2 ounces crumbled blue cheese

2 tablespoons freshly grated Parmesan

5 large eggs, lightly beaten

¹/₂ cup sour cream

¹/₂ cup heavy cream

1 tablespoon chopped fresh dill

2 tablespoons bacon grease (substitute vegetable oil)

4 ounces country ham, chopped

Freshly ground black pepper to taste

Preheat the oven to 375°F. Grease a 2-quart soufflé dish.

Bring a pot of salted water to a boil over high heat. Cook the pasta until it is just beginning to soften to the al dente stage. Drain the pasta, and return it to the pot.

Reserve ¹/₂ cup of the Cheddar. Stir the remaining Cheddar, blue cheese, and Parmesan into the hot pasta.

Combine the eggs, sour cream, cream, and dill in a bowl, and whisk well. Add it to the macaroni mixture. Stir well.

Heat the bacon grease in a skillet over medium-high heat. Add the ham, and cook for 2 minutes, or until heated through. Stir the ham into the pasta, and pour it into the prepared pan. Sprinkle the reserved Cheddar on top.

Bake the soufflé in the center of the oven for 20 to 25 minutes, or until the custard is set. Serve immediately.

Note: The soufflé mixture can be prepared up to 2 days in advance and refrigerated. Bake the soufflé just prior to serving.

BACON GREASE IS USED IN THE SOUTH THE WAY OLIVE OIL IS Italy. To use the grease, however, it's best to clean it. Melt the collected drippings in the microwave and let the solids settle at the bottom of the bowl. Pour the grease through a fine-mesh sieve, keeping the solids in the bowl. The solids can burn when the grease is reheated, but the smoke point of the grease itself is very high.

AGED GOUDA MAC AND CHEESE WITH COUNTRY HAM

Adapted from Jasper's, Austin, TX

Kent Rathbun was part of the group of chefs who made Dallas's culinary scene as hot as a mesquite grill in the late 1990s. After working with Dean Fearing at the Mansion on Turtle Creek, he opened Abacus in 1999, and three restaurants named Jasper's have followed that opening. His version of mac and cheese is made using an innovative technique of actually braising the pasta in chicken stock.

MAKES 4 TO 6 SERVINGS

3 tablespoons canola oil, divided

2 ounces pearl onions, peeled

3 garlic cloves, unpeeled

$\frac{1}{2}$ pound farfalline (small farfalle)

2 cups chicken stock, divided

$\frac{1}{2}$ cup heavy cream

1 ounce freshly grated Parmesan

1 ounce aged Gouda, grated

$1\frac{1}{2}$ teaspoons shredded fresh oregano (substitute $\frac{1}{4}$ teaspoon dried)

$1\frac{1}{2}$ teaspoons chopped fresh basil (substitute $\frac{1}{4}$ teaspoon dried)

$1\frac{1}{2}$ teaspoons chopped fresh parsley

$1\frac{1}{2}$ teaspoons chopped fresh spinach

Preheat the oven to 375°F. Rub the onions and garlic cloves with 1 tablespoon of the oil. Encase them in a square of heavy-duty aluminum foil, and bake them for 20 minutes, or until soft. When cool enough to handle, pop the garlic cloves from the skins, and mash. Set aside.

Heat the remaining oil in a large saucepan over medium heat. Add half of the pasta, and cook for 3 to 4 minutes, or until golden brown. Add the remaining pasta and 1 cup of the stock. Cook for 5 minutes, or until most of the stock is absorbed. Add the remaining stock, and cook, stirring frequently, for an additional 5 to 7 minutes, or until all of the stock is absorbed and the pasta is al dente.

Stir in the cream, Parmesan, Gouda, garlic, and onions. Cook over low heat for 3 minutes, or until the cheeses melt. Add the oregano, basil, parsley, spinach, and ham. Cook for 1 minute. Season to taste with salt and pepper, and serve immediately.

2 ounces country ham, cut
into a fine julienne

Salt and freshly ground
black pepper to taste

Note: The pasta can be cooked up to adding the cream 4 hours in advance and kept at room temperature.

THE DEPTH OF FLAVOR GIVEN DISHES BY A LONG-SIMMERED homemade stock is one of the secrets of why restaurant meals always taste special. Making stocks is no more difficult than boiling water, and it's less expensive than purchasing premade stocks, too. Start with some cuts of chicken, like leg quarters, and simmer them for a few hours with an onion, carrot, celery rib, a few parsley stems, a bay leaf, and a handful of peppercorns.

MAC AND CHEESE WITH HAM, TOMATOES, AND THREE CHEESES

Adapted from The Nook, Charlottesville, VA

The Nook features all-American comfort food, made with only the finest ingredients and with great attention to detail. The ham that goes into the mac and cheese is made especially for the restaurant, near the University of Virginia.

MAKES 4 TO 6 SERVINGS

½ pound macaroni

6 tablespoons unsalted butter

1 shallot, chopped

1 garlic clove, chopped

1½ cups heavy cream

3 ounces Asiago, grated

3 ounces mild yellow Cheddar, grated

3 ounces Monterey Jack, grated

4 ounces baked ham, diced

3 ripe plum tomatoes, cored, seeded, and diced

Salt and freshly ground black pepper to taste

2 tablespoons chopped fresh parsley, for serving

Bring a pot of salted water to a boil over high heat. Cook the pasta until it is al dente. Drain the pasta, run it under cold water, and return it to the pot.

Heat the butter in a saucepan over medium heat. Add the shallot and garlic and cook, stirring frequently, for 3 minutes, or until the shallot is translucent. Add the cream and bring to a boil, and cook until the cream is reduced by one third, stirring frequently. Add the cheese to the sauce by ½-cup measures, stirring until the cheese melts before making another addition. Add the ham and tomatoes, and cook for 1 minute.

Add the sauce to the pasta, and season to taste with salt and pepper. Cook over low heat until the pasta is hot and coated with the sauce. Serve immediately, sprinkling each serving with parsley.

Note: The sauce can be prepared up to 2 days in advance and refrigerated. Bring it to a simmer over low heat. Do not cook the pasta until just prior to serving.

PLUM TOMATOES ARE USED MOST FREQUENTLY IN COOKING because their ratio of solid flesh to seeds and juice is much higher than in other species. They tend to not fall apart when they are simmered, and can easily be peeled with a serrated vegetable peeler. The most popular variety is San Marzano.

ROASTED GARLIC, PROSCIUTTO, AND SMOKED PROVOLONE MAC AND CHEESE

Adapted from Mother's Bistro & Bar, Portland, OR

There's a macaroni and cheese du jour on the menu at Mother's Bistro & Bar, and this is one of chef and owner Lisa Schroeder's favorites. The sweetness of the roasted garlic balances the salty prosciutto and aromatic and flavorful cheese.

MAKES 4 TO 6 SERVINGS

2 tablespoons olive oil, divided

1 head garlic, broken into cloves

1/2 pound penne

2 ounces prosciutto, cut into 1/4-inch strips

1 1/2 cups heavy cream

4 ounces smoked provolone, grated

Salt and freshly ground black pepper to taste

2 tablespoons freshly grated Parmesan, for serving

2 tablespoons chopped fresh parsley, for serving

Preheat the oven to 375°F. Toss 1 tablespoon of the oil with the garlic cloves.

Wrap the garlic in aluminum foil, and bake for 20 minutes, or until soft. When cool enough to handle, pop the garlic cloves from the skins, and mash into a smooth paste. Bring a pot of salted water to a boil over high heat. Cook the pasta until it is al dente, drain, and return it to the pot.

Heat the remaining oil in a skillet over medium-high heat. Add the prosciutto, and cook for 2 to 3 minutes, or until just crisp. Remove the prosciutto from the skillet.

Add the cream and mashed garlic to the skillet, and bring to a boil over medium heat, stirring frequently. Stir the cream to incorporate the browned bits from the bottom of the skillet. Reduce the heat to low, and simmer the sauce for 5 minutes, or until slightly reduced. Add the cheese to the sauce by 1/2-cup measures, stirring until the cheese melts before making another addition.

Add the sauce to the pasta, stir in the prosciutto, and season to taste with salt and pepper. Cook over low heat until the pasta is hot and coated with the sauce. Serve immediately, garnishing each portion with Parmesan and parsley.

Note: The sauce can be prepared up to 2 days in advance and refrigerated. Bring it to a simmer over low heat. Do not cook the pasta until just prior to serving.

SERRANO HAM AND CHILE MAC AND CHEESE

Adapted from Tico's, Boston, MA

Michael Schlow has been a leading figure in Boston's culinary scene since he opened Radius, featuring French-American food, in 1995. That led to a pair of excellent Italian restaurants, and now the group has a Latino feather in its cap with Tico's. The casual spot offers more than one hundred tequilas on its bar menu, and the food weaves together influences and ingredients from many Hispanic cuisines.

MAKES 4 TO 6 SERVINGS

$\frac{1}{2}$ pound macaroni

$\frac{1}{2}$ cup olive oil, divided

1 medium onion, diced, divided

$\frac{1}{4}$ cup chopped poblano chile

$\frac{1}{2}$ jalapeño or serrano chile, seeds and ribs removed, chopped

1 tablespoon fresh thyme (substitute $\frac{1}{2}$ teaspoon dried)

1 bay leaf

1 cup dry white wine

2 cups heavy cream

6 ounces Manchego, grated

2 ounces chopped Serrano ham

Pinch of crushed red pepper flakes

(continued)

Bring a pot of salted water to a boil over high heat. Cook the pasta until it is al dente. Drain the pasta, run it under cold water, and return it to the pot.

Heat 2 tablespoons of the oil in a small skillet over medium-low heat. Add 2 tablespoons of the onion and all of the poblano and the jalapeño chile. Cook over low heat, stirring occasionally, for 10 minutes. Set aside.

Heat $\frac{1}{4}$ cup of the remaining oil in a saucepan over medium heat. Add the remaining onion and cook, stirring frequently, for 5 minutes, or until the onion softens. Add the thyme, bay leaf, and wine, and cook over medium-high heat, stirring occasionally, for 5 to 7 minutes, or until the liquid is reduced by two thirds. Add the cream, and bring to a boil over medium heat, stirring frequently. Reduce the heat to low, and simmer the sauce for 10 minutes. Remove and discard the bay leaf. Add the cheese to the sauce by $\frac{1}{2}$-cup measures, stirring until the cheese melts before making another addition. Puree the sauce until smooth.

While the sauce simmers, heat the remaining oil in a small skillet over medium-high heat. Add the ham, and

(continued)

Salt and freshly ground
black pepper to taste

1/4 cup toasted plain breadcrumbs, for serving

cook, stirring occasionally, for 3 minutes, or until the ham is crispy.

Add the sauce, sautéed vegetables, ham, and red pepper flakes to the pasta, and season to taste with salt and pepper. Cook over low heat until the pasta is hot and coated with the sauce. Serve immediately, sprinkling each serving with breadcrumbs.

Note: The sauce can be prepared up to 2 days in advance and refrigerated. Bring it to a simmer over low heat. Do not cook the pasta until just prior to serving.

NOT YO' MAMA'S MAC AND CHEESE

Adapted from John's City Diner, Birmingham, AL

John's Restaurant was a landmark in Birmingham when Shannon and Shana Gober transformed it in 2004 into John's City Diner and gave both the space and the menu a facelift. The menu includes many dishes consistent with Southern comfort food, from meatloaf and crab cakes to this version of mac and cheese, made with crispy fried prosciutto.

MAKES 4 TO 6 SERVINGS

1/2 pound penne

1 tablespoon olive oil

2 ounces thinly
sliced prosciutto

1/4 cup (1/2 stick) unsalted
butter

Preheat the oven to 375°F. Grease a 13 x 9-inch baking pan.

Bring a pot of salted water to a boil over high heat. Cook the pasta until it is just beginning to soften to the al dente stage. Drain the pasta, run it under cold water, and return it to the pot.

While the pasta cooks, heat the oil in a skillet over

1 shallot, minced

1 bay leaf

3 tablespoons all-purpose flour

2 tablespoons dry white wine

1 cup whole milk, warmed

1 cup heavy cream, warmed

8 ounces sharp white Cheddar, grated

2 ounces smoked Gouda, grated

1/4 cup freshly grated Parmesan

Salt and cayenne pepper to taste

1/2 cup panko breadcrumbs

medium heat. Add the prosciutto slices and cook for 3 to 4 minutes, or until crisp. Drain the prosciutto on paper towels, and crumble it. Set aside.

Heat the butter in a saucepan over medium-low heat. Add the shallot and bay leaf, and cook, stirring frequently, for 3 minutes, or until the shallot is translucent. Stir in the flour and cook, stirring constantly, for 1 minute, or until the mixture turns slightly beige, is bubbly, and appears to have grown in volume. Increase the heat to medium, and whisk in the wine, warm milk, and warm cream. Bring to a boil, whisking frequently. Reduce the heat to low, and simmer the sauce for 5 minutes, stirring frequently. Add the cheese to the sauce by 1/2-cup measures, stirring until the cheese melts before making another addition. Remove and discard the bay leaf.

Pour the sauce over the pasta, and stir well. Stir in the prosciutto, and season to taste with salt and cayenne. Transfer the pasta to the prepared pan. Sprinkle the breadcrumbs on top of the dish.

Bake the casserole for 20 to 30 minutes, or until the cheese sauce is bubbly and the crumbs on the top are deep brown. Allow to sit for 5 minutes, then serve.

Note: To prepare the dish in advance or reheat it, follow the instructions on page 26.

THERE'S A GOOD REASON WHY PROSCIUTTO AND PARMESAN GO so well together. The pigs bred for curing in Parma are fed the whey resulting from the production of Parmesan cheese, and the diet of the pigs influences the flavor of the ham. Most Italian prosciutto is cured for about two years before being sliced.

MAGNIFIQUE MAC-N-FROMAGE

Adapted from Rigolo Café, San Francisco

This modern French bistro in the Laurel Village area opened in 2004. Chef and partner Jeff Gambardella, who trained at Todd English's Olives in Boston and Wolfgang Puck's Postrio in San Francisco, uses *jambon de bayonne* (Bayonne ham) in his mac and cheese, and finishes it off with truffle oil.

MAKES 4 TO 6 SERVINGS

2 cups whole milk

1/2 small yellow onion

2 whole cloves

1/2 teaspoon paprika

1/2 pound macaroni

2 tablespoons unsalted butter

2 tablespoons all-purpose flour

3 ounces fontina, grated, divided

2 ounces Gruyère, grated

1/4 cup freshly grated Parmesan

2 ounces bayonne ham (substitute prosciutto), chopped

Salt and freshly ground black pepper to taste

2 tablespoons black truffle oil, for serving

Bring the milk to a simmer over medium heat, stirring frequently to prevent it from boiling over. Stick the onion with the cloves, and add the onion and paprika to the milk. Allow the milk to steep for 30 minutes. Remove and discard the onion.

While the milk steeps, preheat the oven to 375°F. Grease a 13 x 9-inch baking pan.

Bring a pot of salted water to a boil over high heat. Cook the pasta until it is just beginning to soften to the al dente stage. Drain the pasta, run it under cold water, and return it to the pot.

Heat the butter in a saucepan over medium-low heat. Stir in the flour and cook, stirring constantly, for 1 minute, or until the mixture turns slightly beige, is bubbly, and appears to have grown in volume. Increase the heat to medium, and slowly whisk in the warm milk. Bring to a boil, whisking frequently. Reduce the heat to low, and simmer the sauce for 2 minutes.

Reserve 3/4 cup of the fontina. Add the remaining cheeses to the sauce by 1/2-cup measures, stirring until the cheese melts before making another addition.

Pour the sauce over the pasta, and stir well. Stir in the ham, season to taste with salt and pepper, and transfer the pasta to the prepared pan. Sprinkle the reserved fontina on top of the dish.

Bake the casserole for 20 to 30 minutes, or until the cheese sauce is bubbly and the crumbs on the top are deep brown. Drizzle the truffle oil over the top. Allow to sit for 5 minutes, then serve.

Note: To prepare the dish in advance or reheat it, follow the instructions on page 26.

Chapter 7:

SWEET ENDINGS

There's nothing strange about desserts made with cheese.
We've enjoyed everything from cheesecakes to cannoli and *coeur à la crème* for centuries, along with creamy and cheesy rice puddings that are a frequent memory of childhood "nursery food," if not part of our lives today. Then there are noodle kugels, which hold a treasured place in the holiday kitchens of Eastern European Jews. These homey treats contain eggs, as well as different cheeses.

While we've all enjoyed these desserts, it might seem strange to call them mac and cheese. But that's what they are, and when you peruse the delicious dessert recipes in this chapter, you'll soon see why these should also become part of your repertoire.

RUM RAISIN ORZO PUDDING

A great advantage to making desserts with orzo, a rice-shaped pasta, rather than rice, is that it cooks in far less time and absorbs flavors so well. This is a creamy pudding, with the pasta cooked in spiced and sweetened milk, that then becomes a rich and thick custard.

MAKES 4 TO 6 SERVINGS

2 cups whole milk

1 cup half-and-half, divided

$1/2$ cup firmly packed dark brown sugar

$1/4$ cup granulated sugar

$1/4$ teaspoon ground cinnamon

$1/4$ teaspoon salt

$1/2$ cup orzo

$1/4$ cup rum

$1/2$ cup raisins

2 large egg yolks

1 tablespoon cornstarch

4 ounces whole-milk ricotta cheese

2 ounces mascarpone

Combine the milk, $1/2$ cup of the half-and-half, brown sugar, granulated sugar, cinnamon, and salt in a saucepan. Bring to a boil over medium heat, stirring frequently to prevent the mixture from boiling over. Add the orzo, reduce the heat to low, and cook for 15 to 18 minutes, or until the orzo is tender.

While the orzo cooks, combine the rum and raisins in a microwave-safe bowl. Microwave on high (100 percent power) for 40 seconds. Set aside to steep for 10 minutes.

Whisk the remaining $1/2$ cup half-and-half, egg yolks, and cornstarch in a bowl. Slowly beat about half of the orzo mixture into the eggs so they are gradually warmed up, and then return the contents of the mixing bowl to the saucepan. Place the pan over medium-low heat, and stir constantly, reaching all parts of the bottom of the pan, until the mixture comes to a simmer and thickens. Simmer for 1 minute, stirring constantly.

Remove the pan from the heat, and beat in the rum-raisin mixture, ricotta, and mascarpone. Scrape the pudding into a storage container and press a sheet of plastic wrap directly into the surface to prevent a skin from forming. Refrigerate until chilled.

Note: The pudding can be made up to 2 days in advance and refrigerated, tightly covered.

COOKING IS REALLY PART CHEMISTRY, AND THIS IS TRULY THE case when cooking with eggs to make a custard or pudding. It's really important when a recipe calls for adding a bit of hot liquid to eggs that you not skip this step, called tempering. If you simply dumped the eggs into the hot liquid you'd end up with a mush of scrambled eggs. Tempering warms up the eggs so they are closer to the temperature of the liquid, thus avoiding shock. It also distributes their protein molecules from a tight mass to a looser web, one that has the power to thicken the whole mixture. And the short time it takes to remove the pan from the heat and beat some of it into the eggs allows the remainder to cool below 180°F, the critical temperature for eggs to scramble.

GRAND MARNIER ORZO PUDDING

This light and creamy pudding has the bright taste of orange added in multiple forms, from aromatic zest to intensely flavored reduced juice, and from orange liqueur. It's an option that's never out of season, and is a wonderful ending to a heavy dinner.

MAKES 4 TO 6 SERVINGS

1/2 cup granulated sugar

1 teaspoon salt

3 (4-inch) strips orange zest

1 cup orzo

1 cup freshly squeezed orange juice

2 tablespoons unsalted butter

3/4 cup heavy cream

1/4 cup Grand Marnier, Triple Sec, or other orange liqueur

6 ounces mascarpone

1 tablespoon grated orange zest

Bring 1 quart of water to a boil in a saucepan with the sugar, salt, and orange zest strips. Add the orzo, and boil for 12 to 15 minutes, or until the orzo is very tender. Drain the orzo, and discard the orange zest. Return the orzo to the pan.

While the orzo boils, place the orange juice in a small saucepan and bring to a boil over high heat. Cook until the juice is reduced by half. Add the butter and cream to the juice, and cook over low heat until the butter melts.

Stir the orange juice mixture, Grand Marnier, mascarpone, and grated orange zest into the orzo. Cook over low heat until the mixture comes to a boil. Turn off the heat and let the pudding sit, covered, for 30 minutes.

Scrape the pudding into a storage container and press a sheet of plastic wrap directly into the surface to prevent a skin from forming. Refrigerate until chilled.

Note: The pudding can be made up to 2 days in advance and refrigerated, tightly covered.

REDUCTION IN COOKING IS A FUNDAMENTAL AND EASY TECH-nique to intensify the flavor of a liquid. Any liquid is part water, and by boiling the liquid, the water evaporates into the air, and what remains in the pan are the flavoring elements concentrated. Recipes tell you how much a liquid should reduce. You know the volume of the liquid that went into the pan, so to see if it has reduced sufficiently, pour it back into the measuring cup. If you've reduced a liquid too much, add enough water to make the correct amount.

MACARONI WITH PECAN CARAMEL MASCARPONE

This hot dessert has all the wonderful flavors of a pecan praline from New Orleans. The caramel sauce is enriched with creamy mascarpone, and the topping of toasted nuts adds textural interest.

MAKES 4 TO 6 SERVINGS

4 ounces chopped pecans

1 cup granulated sugar, divided

1/2 pound macaroni

Pinch of salt

2 tablespoons unsalted butter, cut into small pieces

1/4 cup heavy cream

4 ounces mascarpone

2 tablespoons Bourbon, dark rum, or brandy

1/4 teaspoon pure vanilla extract

Preheat the oven to 350°F. Toast the pecans on a baking sheet for 5 to 7 minutes, or until browned. Set aside.

Bring a pot of salted water to a boil over high heat. Stir in 1/4 cup of the sugar. Cook the pasta until it is al dente. Drain the pasta, run it under cold water, and return it to the pot.

Combine the remaining sugar, salt, and 1/2 cup of water in a saucepan, and bring to a boil over medium-high heat. Swirl the pan by the handle but do not stir. Raise the heat to high, and allow the syrup to cook until it reaches a walnut brown color, swirling the pot by the handle frequently.

Remove the pan from the heat, and stir in the butter and cream with a long-handled spoon; the mixture will bubble furiously at first. Return the pan to low heat and stir until any lumps melt and the sauce is smooth. Whisk in the mascarpone, rum, and vanilla.

Add the sauce to the pasta. Cook over low heat until the pasta is hot and coated with the sauce. Serve immediately, sprinkling each serving with pecans.

Note: The sauce can be prepared up to 2 days in advance and refrigerated. Bring it to a simmer over low heat. Do not cook the pasta until just prior to serving.

THE EASIEST WAY TO CLEAN A PAN IN WHICH YOU'VE CARAMELized sugar or made caramel sauce is to fill the pan with water and place it back on the stove. Stir as the water comes to a boil and the pan will be virtually clean.

DESSERT CANNELLONI

One of my favorite Italian desserts is cannoli, with a rich and sweet filling of ricotta stuffed into crispy fried tubes of dough. These tubes deliver the same flavor, but they are boiled so they have far less fat.

MAKES 4 TO 6 SERVINGS

3/4 cup granulated sugar, divided

2 (3-inch) strips orange zest

2 (3-inch) strips lemon zest

Salt to taste

4 to 6 cannelloni tubes

4 ounces whole-milk ricotta

1/2 cup cream cheese, at room temperature

1/2 cup confectioners' sugar

1/2 cup finely chopped candied fruit

1/2 cup chopped unsalted pistachio nuts

2 tablespoons unsalted butter, melted

Bring 1 quart of water to a boil in a saucepan. Add 1/2 cup of the sugar, orange zest, lemon zest, and salt. Reduce the heat to low, and simmer the mixture for 10 minutes. Increase the heat to high, add the cannelloni tubes, and cook the pasta until it is al dente. Drain the pasta, run it under cold water, and refrigerate the tubes on a plate.

Preheat the oven broiler, and line a baking sheet with heavy-duty aluminum foil.

Combine the ricotta, cream cheese, and confectioners' sugar in a mixing bowl, and beat until smooth. Stir in the candied fruit.

Pipe the cheese mixture into the cannelloni tubes, and pat the ends of the tubes with the chopped pistachio nuts. Arrange the tubes on the baking sheet, brush them with the melted butter, and sprinkle them with the remaining sugar.

Broil the tubes 6 inches from the broiler element for 2 to 3 minutes, or until the tops are browned. Serve immediately.

Note: The tubes can be prepared up to broiling 2 days in advance and refrigerated, tightly covered.

Variations:

- Substitute miniature chocolate chips or chopped dried fruit macerated in 2 tablespoons rum for the candied fruit.
- Substitute toasted walnuts, pecans, or almonds for the pistachio nuts.

WHILE THERE ARE GIZMOS CALLED ZESTERS ON THE MARKET that create thin strands of the aromatic layer of citrus flesh, I place it as optional on any list of *batterie de cuisine*. If you want a finely grated zest, use a microplane grater or the small holes of a box grater, and for long strips as specified in this recipe, a vegetable peeler performs the task nicely.

ORANGE NOODLE KUGEL WITH DRIED FRUIT

This is my vision of what a noodle kugel should be. It's sweet but not too sweet, so the natural sugars in the dried fruits emerge as the stars of the show. The combination of ricotta and mascarpone creates a light, creamy custard.

MAKES 4 TO 6 SERVINGS

$1/2$ pound medium egg noodles

3 large eggs

$1/4$ cup ($1/2$ stick) unsalted butter, melted

4 ounces whole-milk ricotta cheese

4 ounces mascarpone

$1/3$ cup granulated sugar

$1/2$ cup orange marmalade

$1/2$ teaspoon ground ginger

$1/2$ teaspoon pure vanilla extract

$1/4$ teaspoon salt

$3/4$ cup chopped dried apricots

$1/4$ cup dried cranberries

Preheat the oven to 350°F. Grease a 9 x 9-inch baking pan.

Bring a pot of salted water to a boil over high heat. Cook the pasta until it is just beginning to soften to the al dente stage. Drain the pasta, run it under cold water, and return it to the pot.

Whisk the eggs, melted butter, ricotta, mascarpone, sugar, orange marmalade, ginger, vanilla, and salt in a mixing bowl. Stir in the dried apricots and dried cranberries. Combine the mixture with the drained noodles, and transfer it to the prepared pan.

Bake the pan for 40 minutes, uncovered. Cover the top loosely with foil, and bake for an additional 15 to 20 minutes, or until a toothpick inserted comes out clean. Allow to sit for 5 minutes, then serve. Alternately, the kugel can be served at room temperature or chilled.

Note: To prepare the casserole in advance or reheat it, follow the instructions on page 26.

RICOTTA MEANS "RECOOKED" IN ITALIAN, AND THE REASON is that this delicate and creamy cheese is made from the whey left over from other cheese production. That is why it can be found made from goat or buffalo milk, but is most often made from cows' milk. It is made by coagulating two of the proteins in milk, albumin and globulin, that are left over when the whey separates from the curd during cheese production.

APPLE RAISIN NOODLE KUGEL

One of my favorite versions of apple pie is made with custard, but it's in a crust. This easy dessert substitutes egg noodles for pastry, and contains just the right balance of spiciness and sweetness.

MAKES 4 TO 6 SERVINGS

1/2 pound medium egg noodles

6 tablespoons unsalted butter

2 Golden Delicious apples, peeled, cored, and diced

2/3 cup firmly packed light brown sugar, divided

1/2 cup raisins

1/4 cup dark rum or brandy

3 large eggs

4 ounces whole-milk ricotta cheese

4 ounces mascarpone

1/2 teaspoon apple pie spice

1/4 teaspoon salt

Preheat the oven to 350°F. Grease a 13 x 9-inch baking pan.

Bring a pot of salted water to a boil over high heat. Cook the pasta until it is just beginning to soften to the al dente stage. Drain the pasta, run it under cold water, and return it to the pot.

Melt the butter in a skillet over medium heat, and reserve 3 tablespoons in a small cup. Add the apples and 1/3 cup of the sugar to the skillet and cook the apples, stirring frequently, for 8 to 10 minutes, or until they are softened. Add the apples to the pot with the pasta.

Combine the raisins and rum in a microwave-safe bowl. Microwave on high (100 percent power) for 40 seconds. Set aside to steep for 10 minutes.

Whisk the eggs, remaining melted butter, ricotta, mascarpone, apple pie spice, and salt in a mixing bowl. Stir in the raisins and rum. Combine the mixture with the drained noodles and apples, and transfer it to the prepared pan.

Bake the casserole for 40 minutes, uncovered. Cover the top loosely with foil, and bake for an additional 15 to 20 minutes, or until a toothpick inserted comes out clean. Allow to sit for 5 minutes, then serve. Alternatively, the kugel can be served at room temperature or chilled.

Note: To prepare the dish in advance or reheat it, follow the instructions on page 26.

INDEX

Note: Page references in *italics* indicate recipe photographs.